STRANGE BUT TRUE
FLORIDA

Strange But True Florida

ISBN: 1-58173-409-3

Design by Miles G. Parsons
Map of Florida by Tim Rocks

Printed in The United States of America

STRANGE BUT TRUE FLORIDA

LYNNE L. HALL

SWEET WATER PRESS

TABLE OF CONTENTS

In A Strange State:

Road Trip Through Strange But True Florida

Florida's official state bumper sticker could read "I'm schizophrenic, and so am I." In a tour from its northern Panhandle shores to its southernmost point in Key West, you'll encounter so many strange and disparate personalities that you'll swear you've traveled through at least three states.

Upon arrival, of course, you'll run smack into the Sunshine State persona. A warm and sunny personality, she's the darling of the state's tourism department. They want you to bask in her abundant sunshine. Cavort in her emerald waters. Spend your dollars at her many slick attractions.

She may be the dominant personality in this wonderfully fractured state, but she's by no means the most interesting or even the most fun. We say ditch her. That's right. Dump her right there at the state line, and come with us on a different tour—one the tourism department will never tell you about.

From the Panhandle's Redneck Riviera, down the tony Gold Coast, all the way to laid-back Margaritaville, our alternate tour will introduce you to Florida's strange and wonderful multiple personalities. Our tour will take you where the kitschy meets the ritzy, in search of the strange, the wacky, the weird, and the tacky. And the tackier the better!

We'll show you giant stuff: ice cream cones, alligators, lobsters, and pink dinosaurs. There's small stuff: the world's

smallest police station and the world's smallest post office.
We've got mermaids and dolphins, freaks and clowns, sunken
gardens and pirates' treasure. There are spooky happenin's and
strange but interesting people to meet. So don't waste another
minute. Settle down, turn the page, and join us on a tour
through strange but true Florida.

Florida, which means "full (or feast) of flowers," was
named by Ponce de Leon because of all the flowers he saw
when he landed here in 1513. It became the twenty-
seventh state on March 3, 1845.

Strange Theme Attractions

You can't lead a tour through Florida without mentioning Disney World. There, we mentioned it. Now on to the good stuff.

No state has a more glorious history of roadside attractions and theme parks than Florida. It began in the 1920s, when mass production of the Model-T made automobile travel commonplace, and enterprising Floridians saw a way to make a buck or two off the carloads of Yankee families tootling down their highways. Like wild poppies, homegrown attractions sprouted along the roadside, luring in tourists with their promise of the strange and exotic.

Between 1929 and 1971, as many as 130 of these quirky show places—strange theme parks, bizarre museums, reptile farms, strange and quirky eateries—dotted the byways from Pensacola to the Keys. The 1960s were the heydays of these attractions. They provided a wonderful distraction for my brothers and me as we sped down the highway on our annual two-week vacation in Daytona Beach, and a constant hassle, no doubt, for my parents. "Can we stop, Daddy? Can we stop?" was the continuous refrain from the back of the station wagon as we read each enticing billboard.

The reptile farms were a particular favorite with my brother, who had an affinity for all things slithery. On many of these farms, you could not only look at these strange animals, but also purchase them (a practice stopped, and rightly so, by animal activists). Every year, we brought back some animal in a shoebox. A couple of times, it was a baby alligator. Once I remember a horny toad, and one glorious, spectacular summer we returned with a baby squirrel monkey in tow.

The monkey eventually landed at the Birmingham Zoo. I think the horny toad died of old age. The alligators, though, those guys may still be around. When they started growing—as babies are wont to do—my brother let them go in the pond behind our rural Alabama home. Although we were supposedly too far north for the gators to survive, there were periodic alligator sightings in the surrounding waterways throughout the ensuing years.

Like those baby alligators suddenly thrown into a cold, strange world, survival has been difficult for Florida's roadside attractions. Their fate was sealed when Disney World (There! We mentioned it again.) came to town. The interstates took folks off the byways, and all roads suddenly led to Orlando. All over Florida, the bright poppies withered and died. Florida Reptile Land, gone! Rainbow Springs, gone! The Aquatarium, gone! Pirate's World, Miracle Strip, the Tiki Gardens, all gone! Today, only about thirty of the original 130 attractions exist. Some of those are in disrepair but still worth a look-see. Many others have been restored to their former kitschy splendor, thanks to concerned citizens who missed the good old days before the mouse ate Florida. And there's more to see, as well. The big, the small, and the truly tacky can all be found on our road trip through Strange But True Florida.

CYPRESS GARDENS ADVENTURE PARK • WINTER HAVEN

Cypress Gardens was Florida's first theme park. Founded in 1936, decades before the term "theme park" became popular, it was the brainchild of Dick Pope Sr. Pope, a daredevil speed boat racer and trick skier, had dreamed of turning sixteen acres of swampland near Winter Haven into a semitropical garden park. Ridiculed for his idea, he and his wife, Julie, nevertheless pressed on, hacking through the swamp on the edge of Lake Eloise and shaping the grounds into a showplace for more than eight thousand varieties of flowers from ninety countries.

Dubbed the Barnum of Botany, Pope was well-known for his flamboyance—especially in his clothing, which often rivaled the vibrant colors of the park's flowers. "I'm not a funeral director," he'd say when questioned about his choice in clothing, such as the turquoise suit with pink and blue accessories, set off by white shoes. "I'm a salesman of sunny Florida, and I like my clothes to match my job."

He did his job well. His salesmanship and public relations savvy earned him the moniker the Father of Florida Tourism. He's credited with spreading Florida's perpetually sunny reputation throughout the country and drawing millions of tourists to the state and the park.

Julie Pope, no slouch in the PR department herself, also had a hand in shaping the park into the showplace it became. Two of the park's most honored traditions were her ideas.

The first came about because of a rare freeze in the 1940s that wilted vines near the park's entrance. To hide the unsightly vines, Julie had a woman employee dress in an antebellum hoop skirt, stand in front of the vines, and flirt with the visitors. Soon, these Southern belles became a park fixture, wandering throughout the grounds, lending a touch of long-ago gentility.

The second tradition began in 1942, while Dick was away serving in the Army during World War II. A group of soldiers visiting the park happened to see the Popes' children and their friends water-skiing in the lake. They mistakenly reported to other soldiers that there were water-skiing exhibitions at the park. The next weekend, eight hundred soldiers showed up, expecting to see a show. Julie hurriedly rounded up son, Dick Jr.; daughter, Adrienne; and their friends for an impromptu exhibition, which was a huge success. The exhibitions were expanded, and pictures of girls in swimsuits perched on the shoulders of burly water-skiers were soon being sent around the country.

Now famous for its skiing shows and Southern belles, the park expanded to encompass two hundred acres and drew in millions of tourists throughout the 1950s and 1960s. Ice skating shows, concerts, a butterfly garden, and other attractions were added. Celebrities, such as Elvis Presley and Johnny Carson, were frequent visitors, and the park served as a setting for television shows and movies. These were days of glory and splendor.

The 1970s, however, brought that pesky mouse to the state, and Cypress Gardens experienced a downturn in fortunes. Both Dick and Julie died in the 1980s and Dick Jr., after running the park for a few years, finally sold it. It changed hands several times before making a 2003 surprise announcement that after more than sixty years and fifty million visitors, it was closing its doors.

Luckily, Georgia amusement park owner Kent Buescher had fond memories of the park. He bought it, sank $45 million into its renovation, and enlisted help from the state. As a result, the park was reopened in the fall of 2004. However, as a necessity of survival, Cypress Gardens has morphed into Cypress Gardens Adventure Park. Fun for the whole family! Thirty-eight rides! Four death-defying roller coasters! The world's tallest spinning rapids ride! Heart-pounding thrills! Southern belles!

Yep. There are still Southern belles. And "gravity-defying" ski exhibitions. The gardens have been restored to their former glory, with a topiary trail, featuring a variety of animal shrubbery (no mice, though), a rose garden, and a butterfly garden. There are still ice skating shows and concerts.

OK, so maybe in its will to survive, this Florida landmark has lost a bit of its weird charm, but enough remains to land it on our strange but true tour. I mean, where else can you find a park whose theme revolves around both bikini-clad skiers and hoop-skirted belles? Don't miss it!

Located at 2641 S. Lake Summit Drive in Winter Haven.

Famous Florida Firsts

The first U.S. earth satellite, Explorer I, was launched from the U.S. Air Force Missile Test Center at Cape Canaveral in 1958.

The world's first scheduled commercial airline flight was between Tampa and St. Petersburg on January 1, 1914.

Strange Theme Attractions

DINOSAUR WORLD • PLANT CITY

In Plant City, you'll find a world full of dinosaurs in Dinosaur World, which bills itself as the World's Largest Dinosaur Park. Jurassic Park it ain't, but there are some pretty fearsome-looking creatures, along with museums and educational exhibits.

Located at 5145 Harvey Tew Road.

Dinosaur World in Tampa is a hands-on, outdoor museum for dino lovers of all ages.
Courtesy of Dinosaur World

EVERGLADES ALLIGATOR FARM • FLORIDA CITY

The Everglades Alligator Farm claims to be south Florida's oldest alligator farm, a specious claim, it would seem, since it was started in 1982 as an airboat ride attraction. However, it is one of the first true working farms in Dade County, opened when the state began to allow commercial alligator farming in an effort to increase the number of alligators in Florida. Today, the park offers tours, exhibits, and educational encounters.

Located at 40351 SW 192nd Avenue in Florida City.

Gator Fun Facts

1. The alligator is Florida's official state reptile.

2. Alligator hunting was a major Florida economic and recreational quest from the 1800s until the 1970s, when, hunted almost to extinction, they were put on the endangered species list. Today, there are an estimated one million alligators living in the wilds—and not-so-wilds—of Florida.

3. Alligators have been farmed commercially in Florida since the mid 1980s and are an important part of Florida's aquaculture industry.

4. Alligators can live to be around fifty years old in the wild.

5. Alligators can outrun a horse for a distance of thirty feet.

6. Wild alligators grow up to thirteen feet and can weigh up to 600 pounds. Their jaws have 3,000 psi of crushing power. Ouch!

7. Although alligators do not prefer humans as a meal, they will attack on occasion. There have been fourteen fatal and twenty non-fatal reported attacks on humans since the 1950s. Small poodles, however, are a favored treat. So be sure to keep Fifi away from the lake!

8. Feeding a wild alligator will remove its natural fear of humans, making it more prone to attack.

Strange Theme Attractions

FLORIDA AQUARIUM • TAMPA

Want the kind of adrenaline rush you'll never get from a mere roller coaster? If you're a certified scuba diver, there's just such a rush waiting for you at the Florida Aquarium. Here, you don't just look at the sharks in the tank. You actually crawl in there with them. You settle onto the bottom of the tank and concentrate on remembering to breathe while sharks swim all around. You can't help but feel like you're on the wrong side of the seafood case being checked out for dinner. But never fear.

The 1,100 glass panel dome of the Florida Aquarium in Tampa Bay houses eight different habitats and 10,000 aquatic plants and animals.
Courtesy of the Florida Aquarium

These magnificent creatures aren't as fearsome as their reputation. They actually don't like the taste of humans and would spit you out like bad caviar if they did take an exploratory nibble. Just kidding! Besides, they're well-fed. Don't scream! And remember to breathe. Just breathe.

For those who don't dive, there's plenty of excitement to be found. The aquarium's "Swim with the Fishes" program provides breathing equipment and instruction that allows the inexperienced to actually enter a 500,000-gallon coral reef environment and swim with the fishes. And the turtles. And the moray eels ... you get the picture.

If you don't want to get wet, you can observe all the excitement and learn about the ocean and its creatures through the aquarium's many exhibits.

Located at 701 Channelside Drive in Tampa.

FLORIDA'S GULFARIUM • FORT WALTON BEACH

Florida's Gulfarium claims to be the oldest continuously operated marine show aquarium in the world. It opened in August 1955, though, so, hmmm. ...

Anyway, the park still stages trained dolphin and sea lion shows daily. The facility also offers swimming with the dolphins, sea life shows, and special educational programs.

Located at 1010 Miracle Strip Parkway in Fort Walton Beach.

Glass-bottomed boats were invented by Hullam Jones at Silver Springs in 1878. By installing a glass "window" in the bottom of a dugout canoe, he was able to observe underwater life, and see fossils more than ten thousand years old.

Strange Theme Attractions

GATORAMA • PALMDALE

Gatorama (We love that name!) claims to be one of Florida's first gator attractions. It may be one of the few that retains some of the Florida kitsch of old. In addition to its gator and wildlife exhibits, the park is proud to offer its Everglade Classic line of alligator

Employees are wary of Goliath, one of the many gators at Gatorama alligator farm.
Courtesy of Gatorama

leather products at a reasonable price. Wallets, belts, and keychains can be offered at lower prices, they say, because the farm-raised hides are tanned at the farm, cutting out several middlemen. Farm-raised alligator meat, along with some tasty recipes, is also for sale.

Located in Palmdale at the intersection of Highways 29 and 27.

GATORLAND • KISSIMMEE

You'd think in today's politically correct world that alligator wrestling would be a thing of the past. You'd be wrong. The sport is alive and well at Gatorland. Established in 1949, Gatorland is a 110-acre park that claims to be internationally known as the Alligator Capital of the World.

Gatorland, a 110-acre alligator theme park and wildlife preserve in Orlando, is known as the Alligator Capital of the World.
Courtesy of Gatorland

Fun Florida Facts

1. Don't expect to see breathtaking mountain vistas. At just 345 feet, Britton Hill is Florida's highest point.

2. At almost 800 miles, the distance from Pensacola to Key West is farther than the distance from Pensacola to Chicago.

3. There are 663 miles of white sandy beaches in Florida.

4. The number of sunny days in Florida averages 226 a year.

5. Florida has twenty-seven first-magnitude springs, more than any other state in the country.

6. The St. Johns River is one of the few rivers that flows north instead of south.

7. Clearwater has the highest rate of lightning strikes per capita in the U.S.

8. Key West has the highest average temperature in the U.S.

9. Venice is known as the Shark Tooth Capital of the World for the large number of prehistoric shark teeth that can be found there.

10. St. Augustine is the oldest European settlement in North America.

11. DeFuniak Springs is home to one of only two naturally round lakes in the world.

Strange Theme Attractions

Lord knows, they've got plenty of the toothsome creatures wandering around. And unlike some alligator parks, where the gators just lie around soaking up the Florida sun, Gatorland gators work for a living.

There are several shows daily where a gator wrangler grabs a six- to eight-foot gator from a pit and wrestles it "Florida cracker" style. OK, we admit we don't know what that means, but it sounds good.

What we do know is that no blood is involved. Forget those old Tarzan movies. Today's gator wrangler is an educator, not a killer. Instead of stabbing the gator to death with his trusty bone knife, the cowboy, er, gatorboy, points out the gator's survival features to the audience, then flips it on its back and rubs its tummy, putting it into a deep sleep. Hey! That really works! A quick tickle revives the beast, and the wrestling is done.

But not the show. Visitors will also enjoy the Jumparoo, where giant gators jump six feet out of the water to snatch food from a trainer's hand. Yikes! No word on how many fingerless trainers there are at Gatorland.

The park's biggest claim to fame is Sobek, who at sixteen feet and almost two thousand pounds, is the largest crocodile in captivity. The park also has an education center, an aviary, snake exhibit, petting zoo, and the Gatorland Express, a train that carries visitors on a tour of the park.

Gatorland is located in Orlando at 14501 South Orange Blossom Trail.

JUNGLE ADVENTURES • CHRISTMAS

Jungle Adventures is another of Florida's original roadside attractions. There are animal exhibits, alligator feedings, a Native American village, a jungle cruise, and a wildlife show.

The park's biggest claim to fame is Swampy the Giant, the World's Largest Alligator Statue. The statue, which holds the park's gift shop, ticket counter, and offices, is 220 feet from snout to tail. It's a favorite spot for photos.

This giant alligator is a memorable site at Jungle Adventures, a 20-acre wildlife sanctuary.
Courtesy of Jungle Adventures

Located east of Orlando at 26205 East Highway 50 in Christmas.

KEY WEST AQUARIUM • KEY WEST

This is an attraction the government built. During the great Depression, Key West found itself going under. Because of this economic disaster, the town turned its charter into the federal government. Believing that the weather and location of Key West made it a grand tourist destination, the government sent the Works Projects Administration to build the Key West Aquarium in 1932. The attraction opened in 1934 as an open-air aquarium, one of the first and largest at that time.

Strange Theme Attractions

Today's aquarium is nearly twice the size of the original, with educational tours, shark petting, and regular feeding frenzies involving sharks, barracudas, grouper, snapper, and other pelagics.

Located at 1 Whitehead Street.

Key West Aquarium, founded in 1934, showcases the richness of Florida's indigenous sea life.
Courtesy of Amber K. Henderson

LION COUNTRY SAFARI • LOXAHATCHEE

Remember those old safari movies? You know, where the big game hunters with their high-powered guns traveled in jeeps through the wilds of Africa? At some point in the movie, there was a facedown with a charging elephant or lion and the poor jeep always seemed to get gored by a big, ugly rhino. Exciting stuff.

Lion Country Safari offers all the excitement of an African safari without any of the danger. Opened in 1967 as the country's first drive-through safari park, Lion Country Safari introduced the concept of the "cageless zoo," where the animals wander free in their natural habitat.

The park houses more than one thousand animals, including all the favorites—lions, white rhinos, elephants, monkeys, zebras, and giraffes. Visitors ride around in jeeps, just like in the movies, but instead of high-powered rifles, they're armed with digital cameras. And no jeep goring allowed!

It also has a petting zoo; boat rides; aviaries; and monkey, reptile, and alligator exhibits. There's even a 200-campsite campground, in case you want to spend the night. You can sit around the campfire, imagining yourself in the deepest wilds of Africa, while you listen to the sounds of the jungle at night.

At Lion Country Safari, a drive-through cageless zoo, you can see animals from the safety of your car.
Courtesy of Lion Country Safari

Located at 2003 Lion Country Safari Road.

MARINELAND • ST. AUGUSTINE

Marineland was the world's first oceanarium. It began as an underwater movie studio, making such blockbusters as *Creature from the Black Lagoon* and *Return of the Creature*, Clint Eastwood's first movie. Unfortunately, the owners were unable to pay the bills making these classic films (imagine!). So they opened the park to the public, staging performances by trained dolphins, whales, and other sea creatures.

Strange Theme Attractions

The antics of those trained dolphins displayed an uncanny sense of Florida showmanship. I remember poodles on surfboards being pulled by dolphins; dolphins playing basketball; dolphins trumping Smokey the Bear and putting out runaway campfires with their tails; and of course, dolphins jumping through hoops and walking on their tails.

At Marineland in St. Augustine, visitors learn about bottlenose dolphins by swimming with them.
Courtesy of Marineland/ Ken Berk

There were whales and sharks too, and stingrays, and turtles, and an electric eel that could zap a voltage meter with 600 volts—enough to paralyze a horse. Cool!

In recent years, the park has closed down several times for repairs, and rumors of its demise have been rampant. Its reopening in the summer of 2005 may have put those rumors to rest. The new Marineland offers up-close and personal encounters with dolphins, designed not only to allow visitors to interact with these amazing creatures, but also to establish an appreciation for the fragility of the ocean's ecosystem.

Located at 9600 Ocean Shore Boulevard in St. Augustine.

Miami Seaquarium • Virginia Key

Opened in 1955, the Miami Seaquarium is the site where most of the episodes of the television series *Flipper* were filmed. Billing itself as "Miami's premier attraction," the park offers four major shows. There are flying dolphins! Fearsome moray eels! A rockin' and rollin' three-ton whale! Comical sea lions!

The creatures' gravity-defying acrobatic "behaviors" (read "tricks") include a "behavior" where the park's star performer, Lolita the Whale, and her trainer "walk on water."

They also have a swim-with-the-dolphins program and wildlife and tropical bird exhibits.

Located at 4400 Rickenbacker Causeway on Virginia Key.

Monkey Jungle • Miami

Monkey Jungle was established in 1933 when animal behaviorist Joseph DuMond released six monkeys in the densely wooded area. His plan was to observe the monkeys in an area that closely resembled their native habitat. His experiment was a huge success, and in 1935, he opened the park to the public.

Now in its third generation of family-ownership, the park is a

At Monkey Jungle, visitors can see four hundred endangered primates.
Courtesy of Monkey Jungle

protected reserve, the only one of its kind open to the public. There are approximately four thousand primates, thirty-five different species, and they all have free run of the place. It's the people who must stay behind cages. Visitors can feed the residents, and there are shows and exhibitions, including an Amazonian rain forest, an aviary, and a wild monkey swimming pool.

Located in Miami at 14805 SW 216 Street.

SILVER SPRINGS NATURE PARK • SILVER SPRINGS

Remember that old TV series named *Sea Hunt*? It starred Lloyd Bridges as one of the first aquanauts and sparked a nationwide—and personal—interest in the sport of scuba diving. From 1958 until 1961, more than one hundred episodes of that favorite show were filmed in the gin-clear (yeah, we know, it's a cliché) waters of Silver Springs.

On a glass-bottom boat tour of Silver Springs, a 350-acre nature theme park, you'll see turtles, shellfish, and alligators in the 99.8% pure water. Courtesy of Silver Springs

Every week, America held its breath as brave Mike Nelson battled bad guys underwater. Knives were always involved, and clouds of bubbles exploded when Mike's air hose was cut—it seemed at least once an episode! Somehow, though, he always prevailed.

Silver Springs had become a well-known attraction long before Mike Nelson discovered it. In the late 1870s, Silver Springs resident Phillip Morrell built a glass-bottomed rowboat and sold rides down the stream, delighting visitors with the view of another world. Hmmm ... so maybe THIS is Florida's oldest attraction!

As the glass-bottomed boat cruises became more popular, the area around the springs was developed. A hotel was built, and in the 1930s more attractions were added. First, noted herpetologist Ross Allen opened the Silver Springs Reptile Institute, which contained snakes, crocodilians, and animals from around the world.

Next came Colonel Tooey, a concessionaire who operated a nearby jungle cruise boat. To attract more visitors to his ride, he tried to establish a troop of rhesus monkeys on a Silver Springs island. Tooey obviously forgot to do his homework, learning that rhesus monkeys are excellent swimmers only after they escaped the island and established troops of their own along the river. In the 1970s, a Wildlife Rehabilitation Program was established to rescue and rehabilitate injured animals.

Today, Silver Springs is a 350-acre nature theme park with a myriad of attractions. It includes, of course, the glass-bottomed boat cruises (electric-powered these days), a couple of historic cruises down the river, a wilderness trail, and animals—lots and lots of animals. Two new features include a ride that provides an aerial view of the springs and a lighted fountain show. There's also a concert hall that features big-name performers. And, hey! The water park is right next door!

Silver Springs is located on East Silver Springs Boulevard in Silver Springs.

St. Augustine Alligator Farm • St. Augustine

There's no wrestling at the St. Augustine Alligator Farm, but there are plenty of alligators and crocodiles to see. In operation for more than one hundred years, the farm is one of Florida's oldest attractions. It has all twenty-three species of crocodilians, a class that includes alligators, crocodiles, caimans, and the rare gavials.

For more than one hundred years, tourists have flocked to the St. Augustine Alligator Farm to see exotic, captive reptiles.
Courtesy of St. Augustine Alligator Farm Zoological Park

The park's biggest attraction— literally—died a few years ago. At eighteen feet and two thousand pounds, Gomek the crocodile beat out Gatorland's Sobek for the "biggest" title by two feet and several pounds. Since his death, Maximo, a fifteen-foot Australian croc, is the park's biggest creature. There are also exotic birds and animals and plenty of educational exhibits to see.

Located on Anastasia Boulevard in St. Augustine.

SUNKEN GARDENS • ST. PETERSBURG

Leave it to a plumber to look at a lake and see a water problem. When George Turner bought his St. Petersburg property in 1903, the first thing he did was drain the lake using a complicated maze of clay tiles. He then began planting a system of tropical gardens in the rich muck, expanding and nurturing them through the years. By the 1920s, noticing how much his visitors enjoyed strolling through his gardens—located several feet below street level—Turner began charging a nickel for the pleasure, making Sunken Gardens Florida's oldest west coast commercial attraction.

The Turners opened a tropical fruit stand and a gift shop in 1924, and by 1935, Turner's Sunken Gardens had become one of Florida's premier tourist attractions. Three generations of Turners continued the family legacy, adding wildlife and bird shows, expanding the gift shop into a delightfully tacky souvenir shop, and even throwing in a bit of alligator wrestling to pull in the crowds.

Like most other of Florida's early roadside attractions, Sunken Gardens fell on hard times by the 1970s. It narrowly missed being reincarnated as a nudist park (darn!), but after ten years of resisting, the state finally agreed to buy the property, making it part of the State Parks Department. Officially declared a historic site, it has been renovated and reopened to the public.

Strange Theme Attractions

The state-run garden is a kinder, gentler attraction. Where is that wonderfully tacky souvenir shop? I remember monkey statues made of coconuts! Seashell animals everywhere! And what about the alligator wrestling? Gee, Pa, I wanted to see 'em wrestle them gators!

Ah, well. Butterflies are nice, too. And there's plenty of them in the butterfly garden. Pink flamingos roam the property, and there's a bald eagle and some giant-sized iguanas still around from the old days. There's a rain forest information center and a children's science center, with more displays and exhibitions planned. And no doubt about it, the sheer beauty of the place makes it worth a visit.

Located at 1825 4th Street North in St. Petersburg.

WEEKI WACHEE SPRINGS • WEEKI WACHEE

Do you believe in mermaids? Yes, Virginia, they do exist. At least they do in Weeki Wachee Springs. Not only do they exist, but they also treat visitors to intricate underwater ballet performances daily in the world's only underwater spring theater.

One of Florida's natural wonders, Weeki Wachee Springs is a natural spring that discharges more than 64 million gallons of crystal-clear water daily into the Weeki Wachee River. Because of the proximity to the sea, the spring and river are filled with both fresh and saltwater fishes and sea animals, such as manatees, turtles, and otters. And mermaids.

The underwater theater opened in 1947, the brainchild of former Navy frogman Newt Perry. Perry was the first to conceive the idea of "hose breathing," staying underwater by breathing through an air hose supplied by an air compressor located above water.

Looking for a way to perfect and promote his idea, Perry built a glass-walled theater sixteen feet below the surface of Weeki Wachee Springs, where he staged demonstrations of eating and drinking underwater. He also hired nubile young women to

The world-famous mermaids of Weeki Wachee Springs have been entertaining audiences since 1947. Visitors watch the show from sixteen feet below the water.
Courtesy of Weeki Wachee Springs/ Leon Behar

perform underwater ballets and synchronized swimming routines. Somewhere along the way came the idea to dress them as mermaids.

Weeki Wachee became internationally famous for its mermaids, and soon tourists from around the world began streaming in. The 1960s saw lines of cars packed with tourists waiting to get in and take a gander at these otherworldly creatures. Eight shows a day, and still there were lines. Some of the mermaids are now allowed to interact with the visitors, an attraction popular with little girls and amorous dads.

Strange Theme Attractions

Weeki Wachee Springs Park is found within the city limits of Weeki Wachee, one of the world's smallest cities. Established in 1966, the city has a population of nine. Its mayor is a former mermaid.

Located 60 miles north of Tampa on Highway 19.

It isn't easy being a mermaid. Not only must the Weeki Wachee Springs mermaids learn complicated underwater ballet moves, but they also must learn to do them holding their breath. And battling the spring's 12 mph current.

Prospective mermaids must first audition, and if accepted, undergo rigorous training to learn to breathe from the long air hose and to perform ballet moves while holding their breath. More than half of the mermaid trainees wash out before attaining the rank of full mermaid, which involves one year of on-the-job training. The final exam is a killer. It's held at the mouth of the spring, where the current is the strongest. Trainees must hold their breath for two-and-one-half minutes, while changing out of costume under the 72° water.

Natural and Manmade Wonders

BIG CYPRESS NATIONAL PRESERVE • OCHOPEE

We've all heard of walking on water, but have you ever heard of hiking a swamp? You can give it a try here on the southern terminus of the Florida Trail. The portion of the 1,100 national scenic trail within Big Cypress is virtually flat for its entire length, and, depending on the season, is mostly underwater up to three feet deep.

This natural wonder, the first National Preserve in the National Park System, was originally set aside as a

Big Cypress National Preserve is home to the dwarf cypress, American alligator, and Florida panther.
Courtesy of the National Park Service

buffer between the ecosystem of the Everglades and encroaching development and pollution. But it is now highly regarded in its own right as a popular destination for those wanting to see its own ecosystem up close. You can do that by hiking the trail or by taking a drive on Loop Road, with a shorter course offered for those who prefer it.

Though Big Cypress got its name from the sheer size of the swamp itself, there are a few remaining great cypresses to see. Try putting your arms around one! Estimates say it takes you and three long-armed friends to reach around one of these ancient trees, many of which are 600-700 years old. Once used for "everything from coffins to pickle barrels," these massive relics of another time are now protected by law.

You can stay overnight at Big Cypress if you don't mind sleeping with the alligators! You don't really have to sleep with alligators, but you can camp overnight and see wildlife that hides from the harsh heat of the day come out to enjoy the cool of the night. Among the hammocks, you may even catch sight of one of the fewer than fifty Florida panthers that remain. Visitors will also find canoeing, kayaking, hiking, and bird-watching opportunities.

You can enter the park by traveling I-75, State Road 29, or U.S. 41.

BISCAYNE NATIONAL PARK • HOMESTEAD

Half a million people a year couldn't be wrong! That's how many people visit the Biscayne National Park every year. The area is rich with stories of shipwrecks and archaeological and historical treasures, but most people come simply because it's beautiful.

Ninety-five percent of the park is covered by water, so most visitors enter by boat. But you can also arrive by car at Convoy Point, the location of the park's headquarters as well as the

Dante Fascell Visitor Center. You'll find plenty of things to do, whether you want to picnic, canoe, kayak, sailboard, or fish. You can even take a tour in a glass-bottom boat, or take a leisurely walk along the picturesque boardwalk.

Biscayne National Park is located off exit 6 from the Florida Turnpike, or south to Homestead on U.S. 1.

The clear water of Biscayne Bay is ideal for snorkeling. Biscayne National Park is the largest marine park in the National Park System. National Park Service Photo by John Brooks

DRY TORTUGAS NATIONAL PARK • KEY WEST

Here's a location for those interested in stories of pirates, buried treasure, sailors, and forts. First named The Turtles, Las Tortugas, by Spanish explorer Ponce de Leon in 1513 for the turtles his crew found (and ate) there, these seven islands were soon described as "Dry Tortugas" on mariners' charts to indicate that they had no fresh water. By 1829, the United States knew it could control navigation to the Gulf of Mexico and protect Atlantic-bound Mississippi River trade by fortifying the Tortugas. Fort Jefferson's construction began on Garden Key in 1846 and continued for thirty years, but it was never finished.

Natural and Manmade Wonders

Finished or not, it served as a Union military prison for captured deserters during the Civil War. Notable among its prisoners were four men convicted of complicity in President Abraham Lincoln's assassination in 1865. The Army abandoned the fort in 1874, and in the early 1900s, it became a wildlife refuge to protect the sooty tern rookery from egg collectors. The name was changed to Dry Tortugas National Park in 1992 to provide additional management and protection of the area's subtropical marine system, including coral reefs, nesting birds, and sea turtles.

The centerpiece of the Dry Tortugas National Park is Fort Jackson, the nineteenth century's largest coastal fort.
Courtesy of the Florida Keys & Key West Monroe County Tourist Development Council.

Activities in the park are numerous. Private boaters can visit the fort using nautical charts showing the route. Camping facilities are available on a limited basis. Visitors may hike, fish, snorkel, swim, and scuba dive.

The park is located 68 nautical miles west of Key West.

EVERGLADES NATIONAL PARK • SOUTHERN FLORIDA

Call this site strange, unique, or incredible, but no mention of natural wonders in Florida would be complete without the Everglades, the third largest park in the United States, outside Alaska. This last remaining subtropical wilderness in the United States spans the southern tip of the Florida peninsula and most of Florida Bay. It contains both temperate and tropical plant communities and is known for its abundant bird life, particularly large wading birds. Nowhere else in the world can you see alligators and crocodiles existing side by side. Endangered species also find a home here, such as the Florida panther and the West Indian manatee. Because of its significance to not just this area, but to the entire world, the area has been designated an International Biosphere Reserve, a Wetland of International Importance, and a World Heritage Site.

Getting into the park through any of several entrances is easy. Detailed directions are available on the park's web site for the route most convenient for you. And once you're in, you can explore the area on land or water, by car, tour bus, bicycle, tram, motor boat, or canoe/kayak. If you'd really like to get to know the area, use one of the many walking trails, then make camp in the backcountry or at an established campground to spend the night.

FLORIDA CAVERNS STATE PARK • MARIANNA

You may be surprised that Florida has its share of caves, in fact, some you can dive in. But this state park claims one of the few caves that's actually dry and offers cave tours to the public.

Natural and Manmade Wonders

Here you'll see dazzling formations of limestone stalactites, stalagmites, soda straws, flowstones, and draperies. And after the tour, if you're of a mind to bike, hike, boat, camp, canoe, or well, just about anything, you can do it here. Stables are even available if you can't leave home without your horse.

Located three miles north of Marianna on State Road 166 and open 365 days a year, though tours are not available on Thanksgiving and Christmas.

Florida Keys

Here's a location that has attracted explorers, scientists, entrepreneurs, and adventurers. It has inspired poets, songwriters, and authors to turn their imaginations loose. And they've been joined by 2.5 million other people a year who think that this 106-mile chain of islands known as the American Caribbean is pretty wonderful, too.

Here you can see the only coral reef in the continental U.S., or take advantage of excellent fishing and diving locations. In Key

Visitors journey to Key West to photograph the southernmost point in the continental United States.
Courtesy of the Florida Keys & Key West Monroe County Tourist Development Council

West you can visit the southernmost point you can reach by car in the U.S., and then walk where the likes of Ernest Hemingway and Thomas Edison walked. If you're a fisherman, enjoy the sea in the Sportfishing Capital of the World, Islamorada. Or visit Marathon, the "Heart of the Florida Keys" because of its location at mid-point in the island chain. Wherever you choose, there are attractions to suit your interest on land and in the sea.

Take 836 West to the Florida Turnpike. Continue until it ends in Florida City, where it merges with southbound U.S. 1, which will take you into Key West. In fact, U.S. 1 travels continuously from island to island, thanks to forty-two bridges, so you can visit all the Keys and not get lost!

LOST VOLCANO • TALLAHASSEE

This entry in our collection is really more than strange—it's actually a mystery that's been going on for years. You see, to the southeast and south of Tallahassee is a large area of flat woods, undergrowth, and swamp. Somewhere within this shady grove lies the alleged Lost Volcano. It's also known as the Wakulla volcano, which is fitting because the word Wakulla is a Seminole Indian word that means "place of mystery."

Depending on whom you ask, you may hear stories about the supposed volcano that spouted smoke every day, or others who declare there was no such smoke. Early seafarers insisted that not only did it exist, but they used the smoke as a navigation marker when sailing into St. Marks. In the 1870s, the best viewing spots were said to be the dome of the State Capitol and the cupola on top of the Leon County courthouse. People came from all around to see "a fiery glow way out in the swamp at night."

Natural and Manmade Wonders

But the smoke stopped in 1886, when an earthquake hit Charleston, South Carolina, and was felt throughout North Florida. People accepted that the smoke had probably come from a fissure now sealed by the earthquake. But smoke or no smoke, people are still fascinated by the thought that there may be a lost volcano waiting to be discovered. A few brave souls, even as recently as the late 1990s, have ventured twelve or fifteen miles into the thicket to answer the questions, once and for all, but have failed. Some barely returned with their lives. The reported volcano, then, remains a mystery, awaiting those with sterner resolve to prove or disprove it.

St. Johns River

Some people say that this is the perfect way to see the interior of Florida, here on Florida's First Highway. At 310 miles long, from its headwaters west of Sebastian to its mouth in the Atlantic Ocean, the St. Johns is the longest river in Florida, and one of only three in the entire country that seemingly flows south to north. If you're looking for a truly "lazy" river, this is it: it has been said to "meander" instead of "rush," dropping only about one inch per mile of its route. Another distinguishing feature is its dark color, caused by the tannin released by cypress trees and other vegetation, making it a "blackwater" river. It was designated to be an American Heritage River by President Clinton in 1998, the only Florida river, and one of only fourteen in the nation, to receive this distinction.

The St. Johns was named Welaka, meaning river of lakes, by the Timucuan Indians. Spanish seamen knew it as Rio de Corrientes, or river of currents. Later, it was named Rio de San

Juan for a Catholic mission near its mouth. The translation of that, St. Johns River, endures today.

Because of its extraordinary length, the St. Johns touches many places in the state. Each offers its own way of celebrating and enjoying this unique natural wonder. Check to see which are available to you, and enjoy!

Sea Serpents and River Monsters

Between 1955 and 1961, Florida newspapers reported sightings of a monster in the St. Johns River. The sightings, which came mostly from local commercial fishermen, described a giant creature resembling a brontosaurus. The creature was even sighted on land, grazing on plants. It was described as gray and elephant-like, with leathery skin.

In 1962, things got ugly. Several scuba divers were boating out to a dive site off the coast of Pensacola, when a sea serpent allegedly attacked their boat and killed all but one of the men. The survivor claimed the creature had a ten-foot neck, a small head, and a wide mouth. Its body was long and whipped around like a snake.

In 1975, another creature was sighted by boaters on the St. Johns River. This creature was dragon-like, with a head like a giant snail and two horns.

Hey, Loch Ness has got nothing on Florida!

Natural and Manmade Wonders

WAKULLA SPRINGS • TALLAHASSEE

Talk about strange but true, but even the name of this attraction comes from a Seminole word meaning "mysteries of strange water." The springs here produce 252 million gallons of water each day, the highest volume of any springs in the world. The enormous source for all this water covers three acres and then opens into a beautiful garden of cypress trees.

The waters here were enjoyed by Native Americans for thousands of years before the Europeans arrived. Even Ponce de Leon visited, hoping it would prove to be the Fountain of Youth. In fact, the opposite was true on his second visit, in 1521, when he encountered local Indians whose arrow would cost him his life.

Financier Edward Ball built a lodge and resort here in 1937, though the grounds are owned by the state now. The lodge features the world's largest marble soda fountain. There are boat tours, hiking, and picnicking facilities, and an abundance of wildlife to enjoy. A glass-bottom boat used when the water is clear allows visitors a glimpse into the 185-foot depths of the spring, as well as the Ice Age fossils and mastodon bones found there. If you don't mind water that is a cool 70°, there's an excellent swimming area. And don't be surprised if some of the scenery looks familiar: you probably saw it as the backdrop in such classic films as *Creature from the Black Lagoon, Tarzan and the Leopard Lady*, and *Airport 77*.

Located sixteen miles south of Tallahassee on 319 and east on Highway 267.

Weird Roadside Attractions

Strange But True Florida is filled with weird attractions—eccentric buildings built by eccentrics, wacky vehicles, way-out places to shop, unusual final resting places, and a variety of other oddities. Come on, let's hit the back trails.

THE AFRICAN QUEEN • KEY LARGO

Bogie must be something of an icon here. Remember *The African Queen*, the clunking old steamer Humphrey Bogart and Katharine Hepburn sailed in the movie of the same name? Well, it's here.

Built in 1912 and christened the *SL Livingston*, the thirty-foot boat once ferried passengers across Lake Albert between Uganda and the Belgian

The steamer from Humphrey Bogart and Katheraine Hepburn's classic *African Queen* is docked at the Holiday Inn Marina at Key Largo.
Courtesy of Capt. Jimmy Hendricks

Congo. The owner of the local Holiday Inn bought the old boat several years ago and brought it to Key Largo. You can see it in dry dock at the Holiday Inn Marina. Or if you're really adventurous—considering the boat is almost one hundred years old and technically not up to code—with advance notice, you can charter it for a short cruise.

Located at the Holiday Inn Sunspree Resort & Marina at mile marker 100.

AMERICAN NUDIST RESEARCH LIBRARY/ NUDIST HALL OF FAME • KISSIMMEE

Who woulda thunk it? Kissimmee is home to the American Nudist Research Library and the Nudist Hall of Fame! Located within the private Cypress Cove Nudist Resort, these two institutions were established to preserve the history of nudism and honor those who've furthered the cause. Cool.

And while we're at it, how 'bout that Cypress Cove! The 300-acre resort is world-renowned as a premier nudist vacation spot. Its clientele come from around the world to bask au naturel in the Florida sunshine and wander naked through

The clothing-optional American Nudist Research Library in Kissimmee is dedicated to preserving the history of the social nudist movement.
Courtesy of the American Nudist Research Library

its 120 acres of protected wetlands. It's just like any other Florida resort. There's swimming, volleyball, shufflcboard, tennis, and golf. You can enjoy a meal at Cheeks Bar and Grill, buy tons of sunscreen at the Fig Leaf Boutique, and tone those abs at the Body Works gym. Yep. Just like any other Florida resort. Except for one minor difference. You're totally and completely, free-to-the-wind, bare-ass naked. And no need to leave the kiddies at home. Cypress Cove is a family-oriented resort, with lots of activities for kids.

You don't have to be a member to visit the club, and first-time visitors can slowly work their way into the swing of things—and out of their clothes. Hey, at least you don't have to worry about what to pack!

Located at 4425 Pleasant Hill Road.

ARD'S CRICKET RANCH • PENSACOLA

"I'll take two beers and a bucket of crickets to go!" That's a common order at Ard's Cricket Ranch. A combination bar and bait shop, Ard's has been serving up beer and bugs to local fishermen for decades. The joint is really hoppin'!

Located at 827 Lynch Street.

CHARLES DUMMETT'S RESTING PLACE • NEW SMYRNA BEACH

Next time you're tootling through this fair city, tootle on over to Canova Drive for a peek at Charles Dummett's resting place. If you're not careful, though, you might run right over it because it lies smack dab in the middle of the road.

It seems that back in 1860, Charles, a klutzy sort of guy,

tripped on a root while hunting. His rifle fired when he fell on it, killing him instantly. Dummet's father, Douglas, buried him right where he fell, covering the grave with a 30-square-foot concrete slab.

Ole Doug didn't realize that this action would pose a dilemma for city officials during New Smyrna Beach's land boom one hundred years later. Since no one could come up with a good plan for relocating Charles when a road was needed through the area, they just decided to route the road around the grave. It's a bit overgrown with weeds and vines these days, but an adventurous soul can still find the inscription on the original slab.

Located on Canova Drive in New Smyrna Beach.

CIRCUS TOWN • SARASOTA

Florida has a rich history with the circus. Sarasota is known as a circus town because John Ringling of Ringling Brothers and Barnum & Bailey Circus lived there in the 1920s. In addition to building a magnificent Venetian-style estate and an art museum there, Ringling also moved the circus's winter quarters to Sarasota and used his circus elephants to help build the first bridge to St. Armand's Key.

Today, Sarasota is known as the Circus Capital of the World. Since 1949, the Sarasota Sailor Circus, which teaches circus acts to students, has been a part of the high school system. It's the only school of its type in the country. Sarasota is also the home to Ringling Brothers Clown College, a school of higher education for clowning.

And that's not all folks!

The Florida State University Flying High Circus, located on the FSU campus, was founded in 1947. The circus teaches ground acts, such as acrobatics, juggling, hand balancing, as well as aerial acts, such as the flying trapeze. There are no animal acts and no clowning, but the circus performs around the state and occasionally in the Bahamas.

And one more. The Tito Gaona Trapeze Academy in Venice was started by retired trapeze artist Tito Gaona, who performed with Ringling Brothers and Barnum & Bailey Circus for seventeen years. The academy teaches the art of the high flying trapeze to adult and children, advertising it as a great way to way to get in shape and increase confidence.

If you've ever wanted to run away to the circus, looks like Florida's the place to go.

CORAL CASTLE • HOMESTEAD

Love's hard. That must have been what Edward Leedskalnin was thinking when he built his love a castle of coral. Leedskalnin was a nineteenth-century Latvian, who at age twenty-six was engaged to marry sweet sixteen Agnes Scuffs. The day before the wedding, Agnes backed out, citing the age difference as her reason for rejection.

Broken-hearted, rejected, and dejected, Leedskalnin came to the U.S., where he bummed around for years before ending up in South Florida in 1920. Still pining for his lost love, he spent the next twenty years building a castle in her honor. Working alone by lantern-light at night and using hand tools he fashioned from old Model Ts, he chiseled huge slabs, weighing from five to thirty tons each, from Florida's coral bedrock. He then somehow levered and dragged these slabs as far as ten miles to his "estate," where he pulled and lifted them into place, slowly, but surely, erecting his rock love nest, always holding out the hope that sweet Agnes would someday come live there.

Since he worked in the dark of night, how the five-foot, 100-pound Leedskalnin accomplished his feat—a task the equivalent of the pyramids—remains an abiding mystery. There were no witnesses and Leedskalnin kept no records. The only clues that remain are a few rotting implements.

The site is a cornucopia of weirdness. In addition to the 11,000-ton castle, the grounds are filled with coral-rock wonders: a Florida-shaped dinner table; sun, moon, and planet fountains; two thrones, one for Leedskalnin and one, of course, for Agnes; beds with stone pillows; and an outdoor bathtub. The entrance gate is made from a single block weighing nine tons. The monolith is set within the walls one quarter of an inch on each side and pivots on an iron rod. The center of gravity is so well-balanced that a child can easily push it open.

The mysteries of Leedskalnin's building techniques are hotly debated today, with many believing his claims to have rediscovered the laws of weight, measurement, and leverage used by the ancient Egyptians. Others point to a picture of Leedskalnin with a crude block and tackle and nod.

However he did it, it's an incredible feat and certainly a must-see on your tour through Strange But True Florida!

Located 28655 South Dixie Highway.

COSMIC MUFFIN • FORT LAUDERDALE

Only in Florida can a plane become a boat! If you're a Jimmy Buffett fan, you may already have heard of the *Cosmic Muffin* from his book, *Where is Joe Merchant?*. If not, settle back and let me tell you a story.

The *Cosmic Muffin* began life as a plane—a 1930s Boeing 307 Stratoliner to be exact—owned by millionaire aviator Howard Hughes, who acquired it when he

The *Cosmic Muffin* began life as a plane, but is now a boat, available for tours and chartering.
Courtesy of Design on Demand and David Drimmer

bought Trans World Airlines. After several changes in millionaire ownership, the plane landed fatefully in Fort Lauderdale, where damage sustained during Hurricane Cleo put an end to its flying days.

The plane became derelict, a draw for vagrants and the curious who would come aboard and lounge around. After several years, it was declared abandoned property and was auctioned off for a whopping $62, an ignoble end for a millionaire's toy.

Oh, but that's just the beginning of the story! Seems Ken London, the pilot who purchased the plane, was an enterprising young man. Hey, so what if the plane wouldn't fly? Bet he could make it float! He cut off the wings and the tail—wouldn't need those any more—and had the remaining fuselage made float worthy. Voila! His plane was now a boat—a wacky motoryacht, to be exact.

Oh, but the hard times weren't over. A few years later, London sold his weird boat for $60,000 and the promise of a Ford Thunderbird, neither of which he received. Unfortunately, the buyer had suffered a massive heart attack and died on the operating table. His estate placed the vessel up for sale, advertised in the classifieds as a true "bachelor pad." (Hey, it was the 1980s!)

Bachelor David Drimmer bit, buying the 56-foot boat for a mere $7,500. The boat was again in derelict condition, and Drimmer, who had no mariner experience, sank a lot of money having it retooled, rewired, and re-floated. It took a year, but he finally moved in and lived there for more than twenty years.

Today, the 65-year-old *Cosmic Muffin* is docked behind Drimmer's Fort Lauderdale home, where it's open to the public for tours and chartering. Through the years it's received much publicity, appearing in numerous publications and television shows such as *Ripley's Believe It Or Not!* and the Travel Channel's *Top Ten Outrageous Homes*.

Open by appointment only. Contact Drimmer at drimmer@planeboats.com.

Daytona Beach Boardwalk • Daytona Beach

A favorite for my brothers and me on our annual Florida vacation was the Daytona Beach Boardwalk. The long concrete pier, which ran parallel to the ocean, had a carnival atmosphere, with thrilling rides, arcades, game booths with chintzy stuffed animals for prizes, picture booths, and even a dancing chicken. (I didn't realize at the time that the poor thing was dancing because the floor of its glass-walled cage was electrified!) There were freak shows, food, and plenty of souvenir shops offering those kitschy souvenirs Florida is so famous for. Carnival music filled the night air. It was the most fun ever!

Today, the boardwalk is much the same as it was back then. The amphitheater, built in 1938 out of coquina rock quarried from the ocean, remains. Of course, the freak shows are gone and so, thank God, is the dancing chicken. But there's still the arcade, now with video games, thrilling rides, souvenir shops, and lots of food. Music still fills the air. It might even still be the most fun ever! For your ten-year-old.

Located between Main Street and Auditorium Boulevard.

> The dance floor at the Daytona Beach Pier is the largest in the world.

DOME HOME • PENSACOLA

Searching for an out-of-this-world place to vacation? Look no further! In Pensacola, for a mere $5,500 a week, you can rent the Dome Home, which looks a bit like it was built by aliens. Those aliens really know how to live, too. There are four plush bedrooms, three baths with jetted tubs, a jacuzzi, private decks, a pool, a fountain—and all with a Gulf view. There's even holographic fireplaces in all the bedrooms! You can have "ambience with no heat!" Just like being on the holodeck of the Enterprise, eh?

Hurricane coming? Not to worry. The Dome Home thumbs its nose at high winds and waters. Its construction is designed to weather even the strongest storms with minimal damage. It seems to work, too, for though the Dome Home sustained damage during Hurricane Ivan, it was still standing when all around it had been blown to kingdom come.

So next time there's a big storm blowing, gather your friends and head on down to the Dome Home for a hurricane party. Kick back with your feet propped up in front of the holographic fire, and pretend you're Picard on a holodeck vacation. The aliens will welcome you.

Located at 1005 Ariola Drive in Pensacola.

DRIVE-IN CHRISTIAN CHURCH • DAYTONA BEACH

Even in our day of pulling in the drive-thru for food, prescription medicines, and even weddings, this site may come as a surprise: It's a drive-in church where you can park and

At the Daytona Drive-in Christian Church, worshipers often honk their horns along with the hymns.
Courtesy of Jennifer Surgent

listen to a sermon delivered from a balcony. As you might expect, services are held in a closed drive-in theater. They were started in 1953, in cooperation with the management of the Neptune Drive-in Theater, sponsored by the members of the First Christian Church of

Daytona Beach, then called the South Peninsula Drive-In Church Service. The property was purchased for the church in 1957.

So pull up and join in the services, and if you enjoy the sing-alongs, don't bother clapping —just toot your horn like everyone else.

Located on Highway A1A in Daytona Beach Shores.

ELI'S ORANGE WORLD • KISSIMMEE

Eli's Orange World is the World's Largest Orange. The giant, neon-lit building was constructed in 1973. At sixty feet tall and ninety-two feet wide, it houses a huge combination fruit stand and souvenir shop and is a local landmark.

Located at 5395 West Irlo Bronson Highway.

FLAMINGO GARDENS • DAVIE

Nothing signifies Florida's ticky-tackiness better than those ubiquitous pink plastic flamingos that for years graced every yard from Pensacola to Key West. For decades, it was easier to see those plastic versions than it was to see the real thing. However, since many Floridians have lately developed a self-consciousness about the state's collective tackiness, fewer fakes abound.

Real flamingos are actually

The 60-acre Flamingo Gardens in Davie showcases exotic plants as well as one of the largest collections of wading birds in America.
Courtesy of Flamingo Gardens

Fun Flamingo Facts

1. Flamingos are born white. They only turn pink when they eat foods, such as shrimp and plankton, that contain carotenoids, pigments that also produce the orange color in carrots.

2. Flamingos can grow to a height of more than five feet with a wingspan of more than three feet.

3. The flamingo's long legs and neck allow it to fish in deeper water than other wading birds.

4. Flamingos can only eat with their heads upside down.

5. Flamingos are very social birds, preferring to live in large colonies.

6. Flamingos can fly up to 50 mph.

7. Preening flamingos often appear to be dancing—a flamenco, no doubt!

pretty rare, too, but you can get an up close and personal view of them at Flamingo Gardens, featuring all manner of wildlife. The park was founded in 1928 by the Wrays, who wanted to create a botanical showplace for tropical plants, which they did, planting orange groves and a myriad of foreign plants. The park eventually encompassed two thousand acres of gardens. When the couple passed away, a provision in their will set the park up as a nonprofit organization.

In the mid-1960s, the park dipped into the tourist trade, allowing a business to run out of it that featured rattlesnake handling and alligator wrestling. There were up to fourteen shows daily, charging twenty-five cents per person.

Today, Flamingo Gardens is a sixty-acre botanical and wildlife park that also serves as a wildlife rescue preserve. You'll find, of course, flamingos, but there are also river otters, alligators, bobcats, turtles, and more than seventy species of native birds. The Birds of Prey center features a walk-through natural area containing golden eagles, falcons, ospreys, and owls.

The park is home to a record collection of the largest trees in Florida, including the largest fig, which is 102 feet tall, has a circumference of 649 feet, and a crown spread of 95 feet.

Located at 3750 South Flamingo Drive.

FLEAWORLD • SANFORD

Want to take a break from the beach and shop till you drop? Then come to Fleaworld! This shopper's paradise, which bills itself as "American's Largest Flea Market," features 1,700 dealer booths that cover 104 acres of shopping bliss! At least that's what three million shoppers a year think. And bargains are not all you can get here. Need your eyes examined? Just see the optometrist on site. Need a tooth pulled? See the dentist. Or if you need legal advice, there's an attorney. And for freer spirits willing to do something really unusual, there's a tattoo parlor as well. If this sounds like a circus, you won't be surprised to know that free circus acts entertain kids of all ages as you hunt for the perfect deal.

Located on Highway 17-92.

FOUNTAIN OF YOUTH • ST. AUGUSTINE

Wanna stay forever young? Then make a stop by Ponce de Leon's Fountain of Youth, purported to be in St. Augustine. In

1904, a tree fell on the property of Louella MacConnell, revealing a cross made of coquina stones embedded in the ground. The longest piece of the cross had fifteen stones, the shorter, laid out north-south, had thirteen. MacConnell, who had said all along the spring in her back yard was the real Fountain of Youth, saw this 1513—the year Ponce de Leon sailed into Florida—as

The landmark cross left by Ponce de Leon is made of fifteen stones on its longest piece, and thirteen on its shorter, signifying his landing in 1513.
Courtesy of the Fountain of Youth

definitive proof of the spring's authenticity. Not only that, but excavators also discovered a silver salt chamber with a parchment, written by a crew member, proving that Ponce de Leon did, indeed, land on this spot. Uh-huh.

So, anyway, you can drink from the Fountain of Youth, view the cross and silver salt chamber, and see a mechanized diorama depicting de Leon's landing. There's also the Explorers Discovery Globe, a lighted presentation on the first one hundred years of European exploration of the New World, and the Navigator's Celestial Planetarium.

Located at 11 Magnolia Avenue.

GRACELAND REPLICA • ORLANDO

Elvis lives! Not really, but if he did, he'd be proud to claim this replica of his Memphis digs. Built about 1980, this version features a guitar-shaped swimming pool, shag carpeting, and entrance gates just like the real one.

The home is located at the end of Hyland Oaks Drive, off Hiawassee Road in the Pine Hills section of Orlando.

HARLEY BURGER BIKE • DAYTONA BEACH

Not much surprises folks in Daytona Beach, but even they might be surprised to see a Harley hamburger tootling down the boardwalk. The burger bike is owned by Daytona resident Harry Sperl, hamburger enthusiast extraordinaire. Sperl is so fond of the great American meal that he converted his Harley three-wheeler into a realistic-looking burger, complete with fiberglass meat patty, ketchup, cheese, lettuce, and tomato inside a fiberglass sesame seed bun. The bun even steams, and sizzling sounds emit from the stereo as Sperl wafts down the street.

Sperl also owns the Good Burger Mobile, the AMC Pacer that has a sesame seed bun for a hood and that was in the movie *Good Burger*. He sleeps in a hamburger-shaped waterbed and has all kinds of burger memorabilia. His hope is to one day open a hamburger hall of fame.

HAROLD'S AUTO STATION DINOSAUR • SPRING HILL

Spring Hill has two unique dinosaurs. One is an auto store and the other is Pepto-Bismol pink. The Harold's Auto Station Dinosaur began life in 1964 as a Sinclair service station—

remember those? Their mascot was the dinosaur that gave its life so we could drive.

Harold is the station's original owner, who quit selling gasoline several years ago and turned his dino into an auto repair shop.

Located on U.S. Highway 19.

HAULOVER BEACH • SUNNY ISLES

Think there's something in the name? Haulover Beach is one of the country's few public clothing-optional beaches. There's about three hundred yards of beachfront here, hidden from highway view by high dunes, where folks are welcome to sunbathe, jog, swim, and hang out (literally!) in the altogether. So bring your towel to sit on, and let your smile be your umbrella!

Located on Collins Avenue.

HIDDEN HARBOR MOTEL • MARATHON

Want to help sick and injured sea turtles? On your next visit to Marathon, stay at the Hidden Harbor Motel. It's adjacent to the local turtle hospital, also known as the Hidden Harbor Marine Environmental Project.

The Hidden Harbor Motel looks like a throwback from the 1950s—one of those mom-and-pop cement block complexes that were so numerous back then. There's a big difference, however. The motel's profits help maintain the turtle hospital. Owners Richie Moretti and Tina Brown bought the bankrupt motel back in 1986 and promptly filled the saltwater pool with sea life for the guests to see. Folks kept asking to see turtles, and when Moretti went looking for some to add to his collection, he was horrified to find so many injured and sick turtles. There were injuries from boat propellers, flippers caught in nets, and dog attacks. Many were also ill or dying because they mistook our castaways for food. Ever notice how much a plastic bag looks like a jellyfish?

Moretti was so concerned that he bought Fannie's, the bankrupt strip joint next door to his motel, and turned it into the turtle hospital. With help from local veterinarians, he began treating the sick and injured. Word got around, and today wounded and sick turtles are sent here from around the Caribbean.

You might be able get into the act as well, for when the hospital needs help lifting and moving their 500-pound patients, motel guests are asked to lend a hand. In addition, you can rest your head easy on that motel pillow at night, knowing that some of your vacation dollars are going to help these magnificent creatures.

Located at 2396 Overseas Highway at mile marker 48.5.

JOSEPH MOBERLY'S CARVINGS • APALACHICOLA

You won't want to miss a stop by Joseph Moberly's to take a look at his work. Moberly, a retired claims adjuster and yard artist extraordinaire, carves really big stuff out of wood and displays it for all to see in his front yard. There are eight-foot tall Indian chiefs and boat captains, giant alligators, pelicans, dolphins, and sea gulls. Just look out for the eight-foot wooden dog guarding the front gate! He's tied, though.

Located at 202 Fourth Street.

Weird Roadside Attractions

JULES' UNDERWATER SEA LODGE • KEY LARGO

If you visit Key Largo, you might just end up sleeping with the fishes. And that's not a threat. It's an invitation to stay at the world's first underwater hotel, Jules' Underwater Sea Lodge. It's something right out of a Jules Verne novel (hence the name).

Once a research center, the lodge is located twenty-one feet beneath the sparkling waters of Emerald Lagoon. Sitting on legs approximately five feet above the sand, the hotel can accommodate up to six people in its two rooms. Guests scuba down to the entrance underneath the hotel and surface in a pool inside. Never dived before? Not to worry. You'll receive a quick instruction course to get you there.

Once inside, you have all the amenities of a normal hotel room, with the added attraction of an underwater show going on right outside your window.

Guests at Jules' Sea Lodge, an underwater hotel, enjoy air conditioning, television, hot showers, and scuba diving.
Courtesy of Jules' Sea Lodge

The structure acts as an artificial reef, attracting all sorts of finny sea life, and it's not unusual to wake up to find yourself being checked out by a pair of colorful angelfish.

Divers can make unlimited dives in the lagoon and explore the beauty of its mangrove environment. Instead of wearing heavy scuba tanks, divers are tethered to a long hookah line at the surface. There is also the option for certified divers to earn an Aquanaut Certificate, which qualifies them for an Underwater Habitat/ Aquanaut specialty certification.

A variety of packages are available, including a honeymoon package, which reserves the entire lodge for the happy couple. Prices are pretty reasonable, too, especially considering what's involved. You'll pay no more than you would at one of the myriad of luxury resorts. And hey, you'll have a much more exciting story to tell!

Located at 51 Shoreland Drive at mile marker 103.2.

KEY WEST CEMETERY • KEY WEST

Everybody wants to get the last laugh. These folks really did. At the Key West Cemetery, you'll find such epitaphical gems as "I Told You I Was Sick," "Call Me For Dinner," and "The Buck Stops Here." My personal favorite is the epitaph given to the local philanderer by his no doubt long-suffering wife: "At Least I Know Where

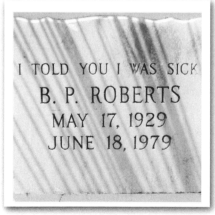

A stroll through the 1847 Key West Cemetery gives visitors a taste of the city's quirky history.
Courtesy of Rob O'Neal/ *Key West Citizen*

Weird Roadside Attractions

He's Sleeping Tonight." That one slays me!

The 1847 cemetery is a Key West landmark and is the final resting place of many Key West notables. Look for the tombs of William Curry, Key West's first millionaire; General Abraham Lincoln Sawyer, the midget whose final wish was to be buried in a man-sized tomb; and Joe Russell, of Sloppy Joe's fame.

Located at Margaret and Angela streets.

MALLORY SQUARE • KEY WEST

Wouldn't it be great to live in a place that celebrates the sunset every night? The celebration takes place at Mallory Square, a concrete pier at the southwest corner of the island. There's a cheerful circus atmosphere. You'll find mimes and jugglers, tightrope walkers, trick dogs, trained house cats, troubadours, psychics, and escape artists.

Of course, there's shopping and arts and crafts. And food. And lots and lots of drinks. By the

The center of Key West's historic waterfront, Mallory Square has unique restaurants and shopping as well as a daily sunset celebration.
Courtesy of Amber K. Henderson

time the sun sinks into the ocean, if you're not entertained, broke, full, and inebriated, then you're just not trying hard enough. A not-to-be-missed party!

Located at Duval and Front Streets.

MS MARGUERITE'S BAIT SHACK • BIG PINE KEY

Hey, look, giant seafood! MS Marguerite's Bait Shack has a not-so-shrimpy shrimp on top of the shop station wagon. It's got a slightly malevolent look in its eye, so I wouldn't get any ideas about cocktail sauce or anything like that.

Located at mile marker 30.2.

NAUTILIMO • ISLAMORADA

No, you haven't had too many margaritas. Well, OK, maybe, you have, but what the hey, have another! Besides, even if you were completely sober, that limo would still be driving around in the bay waters because it's not really a limo. It's a boat.

Captain Joe Fox's *Nautilimo* looks just like a luxury limousine, but it's really a six-passenger boat. You can charter it for sunset cruises around Islamorada, and it's especially popular for weddings. And for that special evening out. Why rent a boring old limo, when you can float up to the restaurant in the *Nautilimo*?

Located at Papa Joe's Marina at 79701 Overseas Highway at mile marker 80.

Weird Roadside Attractions

OLDEST BUILDING IN THE WESTERN HEMISPHERE • MIAMI

Miami is not only home to some of the country's oldest people—it's also home to the Oldest Building in the Western Hemisphere. OK, having said that, we now have to tell you it was actually built on its present site in 1954. Huh?

It seems that the building was originally a Roman Catholic monastery, built in Sacremenia, Spain by King Alfonzo VII in 1141, where it lived happily until 1920, when William Randolph Hearst, who obviously had more money than sense, purchased it for $500,000.

The mega-millionaire had experts draw precise diagrams of the monastery, disassemble it, and carefully mark, then package each stone in crates to be shipped to the U.S. Unfortunately for Hearst, the stones were packed in hay, and upon arrival, fear of hoof-and-mouth disease caused the stones to be unpacked. The straw was burned. The stones were washed and then pitched haphazardly back into the crates, which were shipped to a warehouse where they languished, forgotten, until Hearst's death in 1951.

The next year, the boxes of stones were offered for sale through Gimbel's department store, and in what had to have been a what-were-we-thinking moment, were bought by entrepreneurs (and jigsaw puzzle enthusiasts, no doubt) Raymond Moss and William Edgemon. The two shipped the crates to Miami and began sorting out the mess, a project that took them two years and threw them into bankruptcy. Desperate, they sold the reconstructed monastery to the Episcopal church.

The building has been renamed the Cloisters of the Monastery of St. Bernard de Clairvaux (whew!), although it is neither a monastery nor affiliated with the Catholic church. It's mainly used today as a wedding chapel.

Located at 16711 West Dixie Highway.

OLDEST WOODEN SCHOOL HOUSE • ST. AUGUSTINE

The robots have taken over the country's Oldest Wooden School House!

The mechanized androids, including a female teacher, a headmaster, and a couple of students, greet you at the door and describe a typical eighteenth-century school day. Don't miss Little Johnny, who's been banished to the dungeon beneath the schoolhouse stairs. That bad boy! He never learns!

In St. Augustine, you can visit the oldest wooden schoolhouse in the country.
Courtesy of Kellie Sharpe

Located at 14 St. George Street.

RIPLEY'S BELIEVE IT OR NOT! ODDITORIUM • KEY WEST, ORLANDO, AND ST. AUGUSTINE

Any place known as an odditorium deserves a special place in our Strange But True Florida tour.

Weird Roadside Attractions

Robert Ripley, a famous radio announcer, cartoonist, and world traveler, spent forty years collecting the world's oddities, the inexplicable, the unbelievable, the one-of-a-kind. He began his Ripley's Believe It Or Not! concept with cartoons featuring these wild and crazy people, places, and events, challenging his readers to Believe It Or Not!

The Eye Smoker! He smokes through his eyeballs! The Human Plank! He drives six-inch spikes into his nostrils! The Fireproof Man! He eats fire!

Believe It Or Not!

Ripley opened his first Ripley's Believe It Or Not! Odditorium in Chicago in 1933. Today, there are twenty-seven such odditoriums scattered throughout ten countries. Florida has three Ripley's Believe It or Not! Odditoriums. Each one has different exhibits, so Believe It Or Not, you won't be bored if you visit all three!

Key West's Ripley's Believe It Or Not! began life as the Museum of Torture and Execution, featuring gory exhibits of torture, such as those employed in the Spanish Inquisition. Many of those exhibits are now on display at the odditorium. The museum, located at 108 Duval Street, is eight thousand square feet and houses more than five hundred strange and bizarre exhibits.

You can spend a couple of hours browsing through the strange but true oddities you'll find in the Orlando Ripley's Believe It Or Not! Odditorium. The first odd thing you'll notice is that the building looks like it's sinking into one of Florida's myriad sinkholes. A holographic Ripley greets you at the entrance, inviting you to come in, look around, and Believe It Or Not! Inside you'll find the statue of a 1,069-pound man, a shrunken head exhibit, and a replica of a Rolls Royce built from more than one million matchsticks. Someone had way too much time on his hands! See this Ripley's at 8201 International Drive.

The St. Augustine Ripley's Believe It Or Not!, which claims to be the original museum, contains many items from Ripley's personal collection. Opened in 1950, it's located in Castle Warden, an 1887 historic mansion. There are more than eight hundred bizarre exhibits here. A 10.6-ounce hairball hacked up by local kitty Sashay! A pecan sculpture of the Last Supper! The photo of a boy with a sword stuck in his forehead! A two-faced kitty! Beauregard, the six-legged cow! A cigarette-smoking chicken! How could you possibly miss all that? This odditorium is located at 19 San Marco Avenue.

PANAMA CITY BEACH GOOFY GOLF • PANAMA CITY BEACH

Panama City Beach Goofy Golf is one of the original Florida roadside attractions. At the time it was built, the Tom Thumb miniature golf courses, which had begun in the 1920s, were the going thing. Everything was tiny on these courses—small obstacles, wee putting greens, and elfin statues were the main features.

Lee Koplin, however, was never a small thinker. He liked things big. Really big. So he set out to reinvent miniature golf. His Goofy Golf, which opened in 1959, featured giant obstacles: dinosaurs, pyramids, bright-colored fish, and a huge, kooky-looking monkey. There's also a sphinx, a Buddha, a castle, a rocket ship, a volcano, and a collection of various monsters.

Generations of families have climbed around, over, and upon them. Scads of beer-soaked spring breakers have puked at their feet. Best of all, unlike most other early Florida roadside attractions, Goofy Golf has remained virtually unchanged by the years, despite all the growth around it. So what if some of the concrete statues show a little wear? The kids don't care, and as for the spring breakers, everything looks cool through all that beer!

Located at 12206 Front Beach Road.

PARROT JUNGLE ISLAND • MIAMI

This attraction is one of those bright poppies that sprang up along the Florida roadside during the heyday of family automobile travel. But unlike most, it survived the mouse invasion.

Parrot Jungle Island was the dream of Austrian-born Franz Sherr, a feed store owner who owned a few tropical birds. As his interest in the birds grew, he hatched the idea for building his own jungle, filled with colorful, squawking birds. He rented twenty acres of land south of Miami (for $25!) and freed bands of macaws and parrots as an experiment. Finding that they did not fly away, that indeed, they flourished, he developed the area into a tourist attraction, cutting a winding trail through the coral rock, but leaving the natural flora untouched. Charging twenty-five cents admission, he led visitors on a tour, describing his birds and their habitat.

Today a Miami tourism fixture, Parrot Jungle Island houses three thousand exotic animals and five hundred species of

Skunk Ape

There's a hairy creature inhabiting the woods of Florida, and no, it's not Uncle Buddy off on a toot. Might be Aunt Thelma, though. This creature is reportedly sheepdog-hairy, eight feet tall, and weighs in at around four hundred pounds. Smells bad, too. Yep, sounds a lot like Auntie T.

Then again, it could be the Skunk Ape. Florida's equivalent of Big Foot is also known as the Swamp Monkey and the Bardin Booger, so called for frequent sightings in and around the town of Bardin.

Tales of the Skunk Ape have been around Florida since the 1950s. A particularly intense flurry of tales occurred in 1998, when a local fire chief snapped a photo of the creature in the swamps of the Everglades. Big Foot researchers flocked to the area, and there was even a tour for Florida vacationers to help bait and snare the elusive creature. All to no avail.

The Skunk Ape continues to roam the backwoods of Florida. He's a coy thing, showing himself just frequently enough to keep local interest piqued.

plants. Just as in Sherr's day, the birds fly free throughout the park, squawking, begging for food, and generally making chaos. There are frequent and entertaining bird shows in the park's 800-seat theater, and true to its jungle setting, there are other animals, such as monkeys and alligators, to see.

There's a talking area, where, if they're in the mood, the

birds will speak to you. With a little coaxing and an offer of food, you might also find yourself turned into a macaw stand. Have your picture made with four or five of the big suckers clinging to your arms and head. Just ignore that warm feeling running down your back! What's a little bird poop when the classic vacation photo is at stake?

Located at 1111 Parrot Jungle Trail.

Perky Bat Tower • Sugarloaf Key

If you're expecting to see bats at the Perky Bat Tower, think again. The bat tower is batless. The tower was built back in the 1920s by Richter Clyde Perky, who owned twenty-five thousand acres of mosquito-infested land here. When he learned that bats eat as many as three thousand mosquitoes nightly, a light bulb went off. Hey, he thought, I'll build a tower, fill it with bat guano and ground-up sex organs of other bats, and in no time we'll have plenty of hungry bats flying around.

Well, he built it, but they didn't come. Maybe it was the ground-up sex organs that scared them off. That'd do it for me.

Located at 17075 Overseas Highway, mile marker 17.

Pink Dinosaur • Spring Hill

The Pink Dinosaur lives just a few miles down the road from Harold's Auto Station Dinosaur at the intersection of Highways 19 and 50. No word on its origins, but it seems to be well-maintained, getting a fresh coat of paint periodically.

7-Up Water Tower • Jacksonville

There's a giant-sized can of 7-Up in Jacksonville. The can, which is visible from I-95, is actually a 65,000-gallon water tower serving local bottler SEABEV. The company built the can in 1978. It's 62-feet tall and looks just like a really tall can of 7-Up. More than 325,000 gallons of water pass through the tower daily to produce the company's various brands of soft drinks.

Located on I-95 between Bowden Road and University Boulevard.

Seven Dwarfs' House • Port Orange

OK, we agree, there's definitely something weird about a man who's obsessed with the living quarters of seven little bearded men. But, hey, sometimes weird is good. Back in 1939, Port Orange resident Alfred Nippert felt an abiding need to recreate the house of the seven dwarfs from the Disney movie *Snow White and the Seven Dwarfs*. He ordered his carpenter to see the movie as many times as necessary to build an exact replica of the tiny house.

When the house was finished, Nippert invited Walt Disney to come on down for a visit. Disney did and was said to be impressed. Hmmm … Disney in Florida. So maybe he was impressed by more than just the house. Could it be that Florida's residents can thank (or curse) Alfred Nippert for that mousy theme park over in Orlando?

Located in the Museum Center at Spruce Creek at 1819 Taylor Road.

Weird Roadside Attractions

SEVEN-MILE BRIDGE • MARATHON

The world famous Seven-Mile Bridge spans the distance between Marathon and Bahia Honda State Park. It is the world's longest segmental bridge and is the Keys' most famous structure.

The original bridge, which runs parallel and now serves as possibly the world's longest fishing pier, was built after the hurricane of 1935 blew away most of Henry Flagler's railroad. The bridge was set down upon the railroad's 546 existing concrete piers, and the old rails were ripped up and used for guardrails.

The new bridge, which is actually just 6.79 miles long, sits upon 288 piers and rises to a height of 65 feet at its center to allow the passage of tall ships. The original bridge has

The seven-mile bridge runs between Marathon and Bahia Honda State Park. It is the world's longest segmental bridge and the Keys' most famous structure.
Courtesy of the Florida Keys & Key West Monroe County Tourist Development Council

been the setting for many movies. The most notable, perhaps, was the Arnold movie *True Lies*. Remember that scene where Arnold saves the scantily-clad Jamie Lee Curtis from a runaway limo by grabbing onto her from a helicopter? Yeah? That was the Seven-Mile Bridge they were blowing up!

Bridges are the lifeline of the Florida Keys. There are forty-two bridges connecting more than 100 islands over a 126-mile distance. On a trip from Key Largo to Key West, more than 15 percent of travel time is spent driving over bridges.

Skull Kingdom • Orlando

Like getting your pants scared off? Well, Skull Kingdom was recently voted among the scariest attractions in the United States. You're greeted at the door by the Skull Lord, who bids you enter if you dare, but beware. During the twenty-minute tour, ghouls and demons, both undead and robotic, pursue you through a series of mazes. Eerie tendrils of fog creep around you as moans and bloodcurdling screams shatter the stillness. There are knives and hatchets and coffins and devils and mummies and psychotic maniacs, and scariest of all—evil clowns! So heed the Skull Lord's warning: Enter if you dare. But beware. This is scarier than anything that mouse up the road has to offer!

Located 5933 American Way.

Solomon's Castle • Ona

It had to be a case of, "Hey, Buddy. Wanna buy some beachfront property?" Howard Solomon had dreamed of building a castle in beautiful Florida, but he bought his land in the winter—before the summer monsoons turned it into a swamp. Solomon was a determined man, however, and despite the fact that his land was unsuitable for development, he built a real live castle. The 12,000-square-foot structure houses a bed-and-breakfast, restaurant, and art gallery. There's a moat, a dungeon, and a bell tower, too.

Perhaps the expense of making the land suitable stretched Solomon's budget so that he had to scrimp. The entire structure is made of recycled materials, the most notable of which is the aluminum-printed plates discarded from a local newspaper, rendering the castle a shining Camelot in the glinting Florida sunshine.

Solomon is a consummate punster, and the castle's two hundred sculptures are all some type of visual joke. There's also more than eighty stained glass windows depicting biblical scenes and fairy tales. After your tour, you can dine in the Boat on the Moat, a galleon-shaped restaurant parked alongside the castle.

Located at 4533 Solomon Road.

SPEEDWORLD • BITHLO

A lot of states boast their share of racetracks and speedways. But how many hold boat and trailer races? Or figure-eight school bus races? Both of these strange competitions are offered regularly here at Speedworld, a quarter-mile asphalt oval which lies near the junction of Highways 50 and 520 in Bithlo.

You know right away you're on to something strange when

you see the giant rattlesnake bearing its fangs on the billboard at the speedway. And then the races!

The boat 'n' trailer races are junker boats strapped to equally pitiful trailers, hooked up to stock cars, and turned loose on the track. Sparks fly as the smell of crumbling fiberglass wafts through the air. For a finishing touch, you may see a mannequin fisherman along for the ride, trying to hold onto his catch, during the mayhem. What could be better?

Maybe the school bus races. They're exactly what you'd think: a bunch of school buses running on a figure-eight course, trying to avoid one another in the crossing. Buses are decorated, and some resemble their favorite racing cars. And if you see what seem to be screaming children in the windows, don't worry, they're just painted on.

If you're into the truly unusual, don't miss Speedworld, located at 19164 E. Highway 50 in Bithlo.

SPONGEORAMA • TARPON SPRINGS

Tarpon Springs, on Florida's west coast, is the sponge capital of the world. It's no wonder, then, that the city has a museum honoring this lowly sea creature that gives its life to keep the kitchens of the world clean. The Spongeorama is a delightfully tacky showplace filled with dioramas on the trial and tribulations of sponge diving, billed as the most dangerous occupation in the country. One such diorama depicts the consequences of surfacing too quickly, with a dive-suited mannequin lying on a boat deck, blood running from his mouth and nose. The dreaded bends! Cool.

Weird Roadside Attractions

There's a 1950s-vintage film on the history of man and sponge diving in the museum's cinematic theater, and there are also displays extolling the use of natural sponges. Reportedly, the displays are in much need of repair, but this only seems to add to the museum's charm.

Located at 510 Dodecanese Boulevard.

SWAP AND SHOP • FORT LAUDERDALE

World's Largest Indoor/Outdoor Entertainment and Bargain Shopping Center! Florida's Second-Largest Tourist Attraction! Million Dollar Circus! Gigantic Flea Market! Amusement Rides! Giant Video Arcade! World's Largest 13-Screen Drive-in Movie! Open 365 Days A Year, Including Holidays, Rain or Shine! More Than 12 Million Shoppers a Year!

Find all this and more at the Swap and Shop, a 2,000-vendor flea market and entertainment center. The center was the brainchild of Preston Henn, who originally opened it in 1963 as the Thunderbird Drive-in Theater, the first of its kind on the East Coast. The growing popularity of television spelled bad times for drive-ins everywhere, and Henn, who by all accounts is the consummate huckster, kept adding money-making propositions, the most profitable of which is the flea market. Come and shop, and if you notice one of the center's seventy-eight security cameras pointed your way, wave to Henn. According to news reports, he often runs the joint from his home in Aspen, Colorado, where he has the security camera action beamed to him live.

Located at 3291 West Sunrise in Fort Lauderdale.

The Devil's Circle

Deep in the Black Water Swamp, near where the Wekia River meets the St. Johns River, is an area called "the Devil's Circle." Plants do not grow there, and objects placed within it are said to disappear. There aren't even any insects to be found here. Not even so much as a tiny ant.

Folklore says it's because the circle is a UFO landing site, and that the area has been permanently damaged by residual radiation. Sure makes you wonder, especially since no matter where this kind of circle is found, even in other states, the circles are always roughly the same size.

Skeptics think it's abnormal soil that prevents flora from growing there: the soil within the circles has absolutely no nitrogen, but extremely high levels of sodium and iodine. Of course, it still raises the question of why even those conditions exist just within the circles.

Tests have been done to find out exactly what's going on here! One test involved a cardboard box and a bottle left in the circle overnight. Surprisingly, the items were still there the next morning. But they had been dumped over and moved, with no footprints found within the circle.

TWISTEE TREAT BUILDING • JACKSONVILLE

The Jolly Green Giant could have a feast in Jacksonville. Not only could he quench his thirst with a giant can of 7-Up, but he also could enjoy a giant Twistee Treat ice cream cone.

Weird Roadside Attractions

The cone is actually a building, one of thirty-five in Florida that feature Twistee Treat ice cream cones.

The Twistee Treat buildings, designed by native Robert Skiller and opened in 1983, are 28-feet tall and 20-feet wide fiberglass ice cream cones topped with cherries. In addition to tasty ice cream treats, the restaurants now offer gourmet coffees and soon will add burgers and other such delicacies to their menu.

Located at the corner of University Boulevard South and Barn Hill Drive.

UFO House • Pensacola

The aliens have landed! On top of a house! You once could even see their little faces peering out of the windows at you! (But the new owners scared them away!) The aliens must know something about building houses, too. While most homes on the small barrier island of Santa Rosa were devastated by Hurricane Ivan in 2004, the UFO structure, an actual residence that has been part of the Pensacola scenery for many years, received only minor damage.

Located off Highway 98 on Santa Rosa Island.

World's Smallest Police Station • Carrabelle

This little town in the center of the Panhandle is nationally famous for its police station. In 1991, the station was featured on the *Johnny Carson Show* and later on the television show *Real People*. So what's the claim to fame? Extraordinary police work? Most modern equipment? Most doughnuts consumed in a day?

Nope, Carrabelle's police department is famous for once having the World's Smallest Police Station. Erected in 1963, the station was simply the town's telephone booth! When not out patrolling, the town's police officer would sit in the town's police car next to the booth and monitor calls. Anyone with an emergency could reach the police by dialing 3691.

The town now has a conventional police station, but the booth remains, and people come from around the country to have their picture made beside it.

Located at the town's main intersection.

WORLD'S SMALLEST POST OFFICE • OCHOPEE

This ignominious little town of Ochopee is home to the World's Smallest Post Office. The seven-by-eight-foot steel shed was drafted into service in 1953 when the town's former post office (and general store) burned down.

Today, it serves as both a post office and bus station to about four hundred patrons, most of them Miccosukee Indians.

Located in downtown Ochopee.

WONDERWORKS BUILDING • ORLANDO

No, you haven't had too much drink and passed out on the street. That building really is upside down! At least it's built to look that way. The Wonderworks building is a video and laser-tag game house. Its interactive games challenge kids and adults alike in such educational projects as computer aging and designing and riding your own roller coaster.

Located at 9067 International Drive.

It's Raining Eggs!

Some really strange things have fallen from the sunny skies of the Sunshine State. In February 1958, it was reported that a glittery glob of ... something ... fell from the clouds over Miami. Numerous people witnessed the event, but whatever it was soon dissolved without a trace.

The very next year, a frozen chicken egg fell from the sky over Orlando.

On September 3, 1969, hundreds of golf balls rained down on a section of Punta Gorda. Yes, we said golf balls, not golf-ball-sized hail.

The smelliest rainfall occurred in September 1971, when thousands of fish fell from the sky onto Port Richey.

I'm still waiting for the lyrics to that single girl's anthem to come true: Hallelujah, It's Raining Men!

Strange Statues

Big Fish • Pensacola

Wanna see a really big, really tacky fish? Drive straight to the foot of the Bob Sikes Bridge and there it'll be, pointing the way to the beach with its neon nose. The giant billfish was erected in downtown Pensacola in the 1950s. Then it was moved to its present spot in the 1960s. Its flashing, animated neon lights are purportedly so bright that they can be seen in outer space and are often the object of UFO sightings in the area.

Located off Highway 98.

At the foot of Bob Sikes Bridge, this neon fish has pointed the way to Pensacola beach since 1960.
Courtesy of E.W. Bullock Associates

Big Gus • Panama City Beach

There's a lot of bull in Panama City, and not all of it is in the bars. Big Gus, the Angelo's Steak Pit icon, is a Panama City fixture. Erected in 1970, the 20,000-pound longhorn bull stands guard over the restaurant, which opened in 1958 and is a bit of an icon itself.

Located at 9527 Front Beach Road.

Strange Statues

Key Largo was named Rock Harbor until the Bogart and Bacall movie *Key Largo* was released. The movie was so popular that in 1952, the good residents of Rock Harbor voted to change the name to attract more tourists. Typical Florida tourism opportunism, especially considering that the movie wasn't even filmed here. It was filmed almost exclusively in California!

CHRIST OF THE ABYSS • KEY LARGO

This nine-foot-tall statue of Jesus is located twenty feet underwater at John Pennekamp Coral Reef State Park. It's a replica of the Christ of the Abyss statue by Guido Gallatti, which is sunk in the Mediterranean Sea. You can see the statue by taking a glass-bottomed boat. Or you can get up close and personal by scuba diving down to it.

Located at John Pennekamp Park at mile marker 102.5.

Swimmers come up to an eight foot, 4,000-pound bronze sculpture of Jesus off the coast of Key Largo.
Courtesy of the Florida Keys & Key West Monroe County Tourist Development Council

DINOSAUR ELECTRIC • JACKSONVILLE

Dinosaur Electric in Jacksonville has a shocking mascot— a cartoonish T-Rex, which stands guard over the company's back entrance.

Located at the intersection of Lexington Avenue and Route 21.

FLORIDA KEYS MEMORIAL • ISLAMORADA

One of the worst hurricanes to hit the Keys was the Labor Day hurricane of 1935. Back then, you know, there were no warning systems. No Doppler radar. No minute-by-minute Storm Track. By the time the crew of World War I veterans who were working on the Overseas Highway loaded up to leave, it was too late. An eighteen-foot storm surge hit the train on Henry Flagler's railroad, knocking it completely off the tracks and killing most of those on board. More than four hundred people lost their lives that day, and upper Matecumbe Key was wiped out.

The Florida Keys Memorial in Islamorada honors the victims of World War I and the Labor Day hurricane of 1935.
Courtesy of Jean Eyster

Strange Statues

In 1937, the Florida Keys Memorial was erected to the souls who died in that terrible storm and to those who died in World War I. Beneath the memorial, carved from the coral bedrock, is a crypt containing the remains of many of the victims.

The obelisk of the memorial rises eighteen feet—the height of the storm's massive wave. On its face is a bas-relief sculpture of waves and coconut palms caught in gale-force winds. Close examination seems to show the palm trees blowing in the wrong direction. A bronze plaque on the front memorializes the victims.

Located at 8200 Overseas Highway at mile marker 82.

GIANT BEETHOVEN HEAD • FT. MYERS

Ludwig van Beethoven has often been called a musical "giant," but this is ridiculous! In South Fort Myers, east of

A giant Beethoven statue sits off Route 41 in Fort Myers.
Courtesy of Nancy Hamilton

Route 41, there's a giant Beethoven head. It's made of stone and sits on a construction site. There's a sign that says only construction workers are allowed in, but big as it is, the head can be seen even without going past the "No Trespassing" sign. (We've heard there's also a pyramid there!)

JOLLY GREEN GIANT • PENSACOLA

The Jolly Green Giant is in Pensacola. The thirty-foot plywood replica has been helping sell produce for nearly forty years at Bailey's Farmer's Market.

Located at 4301 N Davis Highway.

MAYTAG REPAIRMAN STATUE • FORT WALTON BEACH

On RaceTrack Road, there is a thirteen-foot statue of a Maytag Repairman. But contrary to other Maytag repairmen who claim to be lonely, this one isn't. He stands atop Andrew's Appliance Repair and is regularly seen by visitors to the store and by passersby. This guy is a replacement for the one that was originally there, but was destroyed by Hurricane Opal in 1995.

POSSUM MONUMENT • WAUSAU

Seen those bumper stickers that say "Eat More Possum"? Well, in Wausau that's no joke. This small town is so fond of possum that it's erected a monument in honor of the greasy little marsupial.

The monument reads: "Their presence has provided a source of nutritious and flavorful food in normal times and has been an important aid to human survival in times of distress and critical needs." Ummm, ummm, good!

The state of Florida got into the act as well by passing legislature naming the first Saturday in August as Possum Day. Every year on this day, the town of Wausau holds a Possum

Festival, complete with a Possum King and a Possum Queen contest. Contestants must submit tasty possum recipes to the judges and don their tackiest outfits. The festival also includes a hog-calling contest, a cornpone bake-off, and the Possum Trot, a five-kilometer run. A good time is had by all, except, perhaps the delectable guests of honor!

The monument is located at 200 Washington Street.

A monument in Wausau, the self-proclaimed Possum Capital of the U.S., commemorates the possum.
Courtesy of the Washington County Chamber of Commerce

WALL SOUTH • PENSACOLA

When the "Moving Wall," a mobile exhibit of Washington's Vietnam Memorial, came to town in December of 1987, it was warmly received and visited by local Vietnam veterans. But as time came for the Wall to move on, some of those who had stood vigil there for five days decided it was time for Pensacola to have a wall of its own. For five years, the Vietnam Veterans of Northwest Florida held garage sales, races, and other fundraisers to make their dream come true.

Finally, in 1991, an agreement was reached with the city for a five-and-one-half acre site to be the home of Veterans Memorial Park/Wall South. Today, you can see an exact, although half-size, replica here of the famous memorial in Washington, the

The 256-foot-long Wall South in Veterans Memorial Park in Pensacola is a one-half scale model of the Vietnam Memorial Wall in Washington, D.C.
Courtesy of E.W. Bullock Associates

only permanent Veterans Memorial outside of the nation's capital to list the names of all 58,217 Americans killed or missing in Southeast Asia. Other military tributes in the park, including a Vietnam-era HU-1M helicopter, honor veterans of all major conflicts.

Located on Pensacola Bay, on Bayfront Parkway and 9th Avenue.

WORLD'S LARGEST LOBSTER • ISLAMORADA

Yikes! It's the invasion of the giant lobsters! Oh, wait. There's just one. But it's a really big one! The World's Largest Lobster stands guard outside Treasure Village, a small shopping area on Islamorada. The 35-foot lobster is creepily lifelike. It's not hard to imagine it suddenly coming to life and attacking like the monsters in one of those B movies of old. It's definitely worth a look-see. Oh, yeah, and while you're there, you might as well check out the shopping center.

Located at 86729 Old Highway at mile marker 86.7.

WORLD'S SECOND-LARGEST GATOR • KISSIMMEE

The World's Second-Largest Gator statue (remember, the largest is located at Jungle Adventures in Christmas) is here! The 126-foot-long gator is seen crunching onto a safari jeep, with a hapless guide hanging on for dear life. The statue once stood guard at the gates of Jungleland Zoo, but when that venerable park closed in 2002, the giant gator was left behind. Luckily, it sits adjacent to the aptly named Gator Motel.

Located at 4576 West Irlo Bronson Highway.

In 1937, Amelia Earhart took off from Miami for an around-the-world flight and was never seen again.

Strange Museums

AMERICAN POLICE HALL OF FAME AND MUSEUM • TITUSVILLE

OK, maybe you wouldn't think that the American Police Hall of Fame and Museum would qualify for our tour. Oh, but you'd be so wrong! Inside the museum are more than ten thousand exhibits detailing the history of law enforcement in the U.S. And a grisly history it's been. You'll see human skulls with entry wounds, gruesome crime scene photos, and then there's the capital punishment exhibit, including an actual guillotine, an electric chair, and a gas chamber.

Many of the displays are interactive, allowing you to actually feel what it's like to investigate a crime scene, to be sitting on death row, or to be strapped into the electric chair. You can even have your picture made wearing

At the American Police Hall of Fame in Titusville, visitors discover law enforcement history and remember those lost in the line of duty.
Courtesy of the American Police Hall of Fame/ Peter Connolly

stripes to send to the folks back home. They also have a gun range open to the public, and they offer helicopter rides.

Strange Museums

Although the museum is morbid fun for all of us strange but true tourists, it is also a solemn memorial to the more than 7,500 police officers who have died in the line of duty. Each officer's name, rank, and hometown are carved into a massive marble monument. There's also a memorial to the K-9 officers who have died on duty.

Located at Vectorspace Boulevard and Route 1.

American Water Ski Experience Hall of Fame Museum • Polk City

Many people mistakenly believe that Dick Pope Sr., founder of Cypress Gardens, invented water-skiing. Not so! The sport was invented by Minnesota teenager Ralph Samuelson on June 28, 1922, when he strapped two boards on his feet and had a friend pull him behind his boat.

Samuelson is honored as the inventor at the American Water Ski Experience Hall of Fame Museum in Polk City, where his statue greets you at the entryway. Enthusiasts will enjoy a visit to the museum, where exhibits depict the advancement of water-skiing as a sport, including the introduction of barefooting, jumping, pyramids, swivel skiing, and other stunts. There's a display of skis through the years and biographies on pioneers, such as Pope, who was dubbed the Swami of the Swamp.

Located at 1251 Holy Cow Road (worth a visit just for that street name!) in Polk City.

CRYSTAL ICE HOUSE • PENSACOLA

The Crystal Ice House is a relic of days gone by. Built in 1932, it's the last remaining of four architecturally-unique ice distribution houses. The small house built of concrete has concrete icicles jutting around the eaves. In finishing the building, mica was mixed into the paint, so that the entire structure shimmers and shines in the Florida sunshine. Set into the wall is an original stone slab that reads "Hand Signals For Service." It shows two fingers for twenty-five pounds, three for fifty pounds, and so on.

The house, recently restored by Pensacola's historical society, is located at 2024 North Davis Street.

HOLY LAND EXPERIENCE • ORLANDO

With all due respect, this may at first seem like a theme park, but it's actually a museum of the biblical kind. Its web site boasts, "It has been 2000 years since the world has seen anything like this!" Sure enough, it offers sights, sounds, and even tastes you would have found in biblical days gone by.

From the moment you pass through the gates

Praise Through the Ages is just one of the musical presentations at the Holy Land Experience.
Courtesy of The Holy Land Experience

of the "walled city," you'll think you are in ancient Jerusalem. Structures and exhibits show in amazing detail the architecture, settings, and lifestyle of the Holy Land 2000 years ago. Visit replicas of the Garden Tomb and the Wilderness Tabernacle. Step under the massive archway that enters into the spectacular Plaza of Nations. Or visit the Scriptorium: Center for Biblical Antiquities, which houses the finest private collection of authentic biblical artifacts and antiquities in the world. See up close ancient scrolls, manuscripts, and Bibles you won't see anywhere else. And to complete your experience, dramatic presentations throughout your visit will make the Holy Land truly come alive.

Located alongside I-4, exit 78, at the corner of Conroy and Vineland Roads, immediately off the exit ramp.

Liberty Bell Memorial Museum • Melbourne

Feeling patriotic on your visit to strange but true Florida? Then you'll want to see the Liberty Bell Memorial Museum, which represents more than three hundred years of United States history. As the name suggests, its centerpiece is a full-size replica of the original Liberty Bell. Cast by Whitechapel Foundry in London, England—makers of the original bell—this authentic recreation is one of only twenty-five known to exist in the world.

The story of how the bell came to be in Florida is a little strange in itself. As preparations were being made for our nation's bicentennial, one hundred full-size, uncracked replicas of the original Liberty Bell were made with the intention of allowing each state to have two. Disney was the first to submit a request for one of the Florida bells, but was turned down because the replicas were only to go to nonprofit organizations.

The Liberty Bell Memorial Museum houses a full-size replica of the original Liberty Bell, cast by the maker of the original.
Courtesy of the Liberty Bell Memorial Museum

However, there was a fee involved, which the school children of South Brevard County raised, and so the bell came here. It is not known whether Florida's other designated bell was actually claimed. But you can see this one, and even tap it with a rubber mallet to let freedom ring!

While you're there, you can also see artifacts and memorabilia from all American wars, military weapons and clothing, replicas of historical documents, and a gallery of U.S. flags. Paintings and photos of presidents and historic events line the walls. Oh, and be sure and notice the museum itself while you're there—it's a remodeled ground water tank!

The museum is located at 1601 Oak Street in Melbourne.

Strange Museums

MEL FISHER MARITIME HERITAGE SOCIETY MUSEUM • KEY WEST

"Today's the Day!" This was treasure salvor Mel Fisher's daily cry as he and his crew of treasure hunters searched for sunken treasure off the shores of the Florida Keys. Fisher had chosen Florida for his search in the 1960s because the waters surrounding the area were reputed to be filled with the wrecks of Spanish galleons, many of which were said to be laden with gold, silver, precious gems, and other such treasures.

Employing his family and a group of like-minded divers, Fisher became obsessed with the hunt for treasure. A pioneer in the field of treasure salvage, he and his group are responsible for many innovations in equipment and techniques that are used routinely today.

The group's first Florida find was the treasure fleet of 1715, sunk off the coast of Fort Pierce. While working the wreck, Fisher uncovered a cache of coins, thousands of them scattered like a carpet of gold on the seabed—a sight never to be forgotten, said Fisher. Duh!

The find triggered a gold rush of divers to the site, and the state of Florida, wanting some of the action, passed legislation requiring that salvors relinquish 25 percent of their find to the state.

Despite the success of his group, which continued to bring up fortunes in gold, silver, and jewelry all along the Florida coast, Fisher wasn't satisfied. He was obsessed with striking the mother lode, a treasure ship laden with riches beyond even his wildest dreams. He knew it was down there. He even knew its name.

On September 4, 1622, the Tierra Firma flota, a fleet of Spanish ships, left Havana delivering untold wealth plundered from ancient empires. There was Mexican and Peruvian silver, gold and emeralds from Columbia, pearls from Venezuela.

Reportedly, the galleon *Nuestra Senora de Atocha* was the richest of the fleet's twenty-eight ships. The wealth it held was almost beyond belief: twenty-four tons of silver bullion in 1,038 ingots, 180,000 pesos of silver coins, 582 copper ingots, 125 gold bars and discs, twenty chests of indigo, and 1,200 pounds of silverware. And this did not include items such as untold millions in emeralds and jewelry that were being smuggled to avoid taxation.

Just two days out of Havana, a hurricane hit, sinking the *Atocha* and seven other ships in the fleet and scattering their riches along the seabed from the Marquesas Keys to the Dry Tortugas.

Word of the *Atocha* reached Mel Fisher in 1969, and he knew this was it. This

At the Mel Fisher Museum, visitors discover recovered artifacts from shipwrecks off the Key West coast.
Courtesy of Kevin Henderson

ship was his mother lode. It became his obsession. His quest. To find the ship and bring her treasure up from the bottom of the sea.

Strange Museums

For sixteen years, Fisher and his group, Treasure Salvors, relentlessly searched for the *Atocha*. Along the way, they uncovered other ships in the fleet and brought up other treasures, but for Fisher, it wasn't enough. The *Atocha* was down there, and he was going to find it.

Finally in 1973, after an exhaustive search, three silver bars were found that matched the tally numbers on the *Atocha's* manifest. This was it. He had found his wreck. The *Atocha* wasn't going to give up her treasure easily, however. It had languished on the bottom for centuries, and it would still take Fisher years to uncover it.

In 1975, Fisher lost a son, a daughter-in-law, and a good friend when their boat, anchored on the salvage site, capsized in a hurricane. But, still, Fisher pressed on. Ten more long, hard years passed, but he never gave up, rising every day to give his proclamation: Today's the Day!

July 20, 1985 was the day. On that day, ecstatic crew members found themselves swimming over a reef of silver bars. They had hit the mother lode.

Today, many of the riches of the *Atocha* and other fleet ships can be seen at the Mel Fisher Maritime Heritage Society Museum. A fortune in silver and gold bars. A solid gold belt and necklace set with precious gems. A gold chalice designed to protect its user from poisoning. A seven-pound gold chain. A six-inch gold cross set with emeralds. And that's only a sample.

In addition to gold and jewels, the museum features everyday items that have been preserved from the ship. Treasure Salvors continues to excavate the site, and new items, both the mundane and the spectacular, are constantly added.

The museum is open 365 days a year. In addition to getting a close-up view of riches beyond your wildest dreams, there are video presentations documenting the search for the *Atocha* and other exhibits. In the museum's store, you can purchase your own piece of treasure—a coin from the *Atocha*.

Located at 200 Greene Street.

The Florida Panhandle was nicknamed The Miracle Strip during the 1950s through the 1970s. The strip began at Panama City Beach and stretched west through Destin, Fort Walton, and Pensacola. The area earned its name because of the beauty of the white-sand beaches contrasting with the blue water of the Gulf of Mexico.

Years ago, the area billed itself as having the World's Whitest Beaches, a not-so-specious claim. Unlike sand on other beaches, which is made from pulverized shell, the sand of the Panhandle's beaches is 99 percent pure quartz, formed in the Appalachian Mountains.

MUSEUM OF SCIENCE AND INDUSTRY • TAMPA

A very large red dinosaur stands outside the Museum of Science and Industry in Tampa. There are even more dinos inside—sauropods, it seems. The museum is one of the few in the world to display these dinosaurs, which are some of the largest articulated dinosaurs ever discovered.

The museum is located at 4801 East Fowler Avenue.

Strange Museums

MUSEUM OF THE MAN-IN-THE-SEA • PANAMA CITY BEACH

The Museum of the Man-In-The-Sea is a study in weird stuff. It's chocked to the gills with memorabilia from man's early days of underwater exploration, beginning with the earliest attempt to breathe underwater from animal-skin bladders. Yuck! The museum is internationally famous for its comprehensive collection of firsts in underwater technology, including scuba gear, submersibles, and commercial diving suits. Also on display are now unsunken treasures, such as gold ingots, jewelry, silver plates, shells, and bottles.

Located at 17314 Panama City Beach Parkway.

POTTER'S WAX MUSEUM • ST. AUGUSTINE

Potter's Wax Museum was the first wax museum to open in the United States. It's one of the few remaining today. George L. Potter opened the museum in 1949, flying many of his wax figures from Europe on commercial flights—sitting in their own seats. When he died in 1980, the museum was sold to its present owner and moved to a smaller location.

Today, 160 figures, including such historical figures as Thomas Jefferson, Ben Franklin, Leonardo da Vinci, and Queen Victoria, are showcased in small galleries. There's also plenty of contemporary history to see too, what with Princess Di, Arnold Schwarzenegger, Britney Spears, and the cast of *Seinfeld* hanging around. And don't miss the Chamber of Horrors, where the fake blood flows freely.

Located at 17 King Street.

PRESIDENTS HALL OF FAME • CLERMONT

Visiting the Presidents Hall of Fame is like taking a step back into the days of the old Florida tourism. The wax presidential figures are reportedly showing some wear: a bit of sagging, some fingers missing here and there, and at one point, visitors found President Clinton had toppled (no report on where Monica was at the time).

The Presidents Hall of Fame contains artifacts from all U.S. presidents and first ladies.
Photo courtesy of Presidents Hall of Fame

The museum, which opened in 1962 as the House of Presidents, contains artifacts from all forty-three presidents and first ladies. You'll find inaugural ball gowns, china, and Christmas cards and ornaments, among other things. One of the most bizarre displays is the replica of Abe Lincoln's face and hands, made in 1860. There's also a replica of the Lincoln monument at the entrance to the museum.

Jack Zweifel's miniature replica of the White House, which he spent the last forty years constructing, is also here. Zweifel first gained permission from President John F. Kennedy to build the replica in 1962, but it was 1975 before he was allowed inside to take measurements and photographs for the planned model.

Since that time, he, his wife, his family, and thousands of volunteers have produced a sixty-foot long, twenty-foot wide exact replica built on a scale of one inch to one foot. So exacting is Zweifel about his White House that he has included everything, even the cracks in the ceiling and the coffee stains on the rugs. He calls the White House curator every few weeks for an update on any small mishaps that may have occurred and immediately adds them.

The model is an amazing creation. Every stick of furniture is made to scale and is constructed from the same type of wood as the original. Rugs and fabrics are hand stitched; portraits are painted in miniature. And everything works, including toilets, computers, TVs, and telephones.

The replica weighs ten tons, but that doesn't keep Zweifel from sharing his creation with the world. He just loads it onto a semi and travels around the country with it. When the replica is not traveling, it's housed here at the museum.

Located at 123 North U.S. Highway 27.

T.T. Wentworth Jr. Florida State Museum • Pensacola

The T.T. Wentworth Jr. Florida State Museum is an original Florida roadside attraction that, despite its move to downtown Pensacola, has retained some of its old-time kitschy charm. Opened in 1957 by Ripley-wannabe T. T. Wentworth Jr., the museum has four floors of oddities, including vintage bottles and vending machines, World War II items, commemorative plates, and the world's tallest man's shoe (size 37!). One of the favorite displays is a petrified kitty, which, it seems, was accidentally

The Historic Pensacola Village and the T.T. Wentworth Jr. Florida State Museum houses 67,000 objects of historical value to Pensacola and Escambia County.
Courtesy of the West Florida Historic Preservation, Inc.

sealed into a wall in 1850 and not discovered until remodeling took place in 1946. Wentworth would be pleased to see that at least this icky oddity has survived the PC world. Unfortunately, his display of shrunken heads wasn't so lucky.

Located at 330 Jefferson Street.

WORLD'S LARGEST GONE WITH THE WIND COLLECTION • PLANT CITY

"Frankly, my dear," this spot is for our die-hard *Gone with the Wind* fans. It's all about the famous movie and anything connected to it. Enjoy a guided tour or browse at your leisure. Shop at the collectibles shop, which offers the widest selection of *GWTW* items in the world, and see the *GWTW* Character Doll Gallery. The collection is normally open only Tuesday through Saturday of each week, but if those days aren't convenient, don't "think about it tomorrow"; call for a before/after hours appointment.

Located at Walden Lake, 1701 Alexander Street, Suite 112-1.

Weeping Icon

On December 6, 1970, at the St. Nicholas Greek Orthodox Cathedral in Tarpon Springs, a woman cleaning the church noticed something odd about the icon of the church's patron saint, St. Nicholas: drops of moisture had formed around the eyes in his image. A carpenter was even called in to assure that the structure was airtight. But the droplets continued.

The icon "cried" for three years, finally stopping on December 8, 1973. Nothing else happened until August of 1992, when St. Nicholas began to cry again. His last tear fell on February 15, 1996, though dried tear tracks can be seen in the glass covering the icon.

The Haunting of Florida

Mist rising on moonlit nights. Ghostly apparitions floating through hallowed halls. Strange and scary noises. Florida can be a spooky place at night. With such a wild and varied history, it's no wonder there are haints wandering the land. Here's just a smattering of Florida's legendary ghost tales.

AL CAPONE'S HOME • SORRENTO

Ever thought you might want to get in bed with the mob? The residents of Al Capone's home in Sorrento may have had that peculiar experience. Reportedly, the beautiful Victorian-style home where Al Capone lived out his last days is haunted by the old gangster. Many residents have been frightened by pots and pans banging in the night, lights turning on and off—and the feeling that someone is crawling into the bed with them!

ANASTASIA ISLAND LIGHTHOUSE • ANASTASIA ISLAND

The Lighthouse on Anastasia Island is quite a crowded place—for ghosts, that is. Workers who were restoring the lighthouse in the 1980s reported seeing the apparition of a man hanging from a rafter. They heard footsteps on the stairs when no one was around and reported an uneasy feeling in the cellar, though no one reported seeing a ghost there.

The most interesting spirit is the little girl, dressed in 1800s-era clothing. She would appear to the men at night, then disappear. She's believed to be one of two little girl spirits, both daughters of a former lighthouse keeper. It seems the two girls were playing in a train cart that was used to haul supplies. The brake loosened, and the train cart plunged into the sea, drowning the girls. Occasionally, little-girl giggles can be heard around the lighthouse, and the bolder of the two periodically appears to visitors.

St. Augustine, Daytona Beach, Orlando, and Key West offer guided ghost tours. On these tours, you're guided through the town's spookiest buildings and cemeteries in search of the supernatural. Along the way, you learn of the town's history and get to experience a delicious thrill of fear.

Britton Cinema • Tampa

OK. Here's one that'll scare the pee out of you. At the Britton Cinema, female patrons have reported that the stalls in the ladies room will shut and lock, and the toilets will flush of their own accord.

Located at 3938 S. Dale Mabry Highway.

Casablanca Inn • St. Augustine

During Prohibition, St. Augustine was a hub of smuggling. Most of the illegal rum smuggled into the U.S. from Cuba entered along the St. Augustine waterfront. The Casablanca Inn, then known as the elegant Matanzas Hotel, was owned by an enterprising widow, whose high breeding hid an adventurous soul tinged with a bit of larceny.

The good widow took up with a group of rumrunners, one of whom became her lover. The smugglers set up a secret shop in her boarding house, selling liquor to the guests and locals they could trust. They would stay until the liquor was gone, then they'd head back out to sea for another shipment.

The government men were suspicious of the inn and questioned the widow, but she remained mum about her activities. If the G-men were in town when the bootleggers returned, she devised a signal where she would climb to the roof of the building and wave a lantern back and forth. Seeing the signal, the bootleggers would bypass her property and sail safely into the St. Augustine waterfront farther down. Once the coast was clear, they would once again set up shop at the inn, and the widow would reap the rewards.

The widow is said to be sending her signal yet today. Guests of properties adjacent to the Casablanca Inn report being awakened by light shining into their windows. Thinking it to be the lighthouse on Anastasia Island, they peer out the window only to see that the light is coming from the roof of the Casablanca Inn. Many a crew of local shrimp boats and other watercraft report entering the inlet to see an eerie lantern light swinging above the Casablanca Inn. Some even swear they've seen the outline of a dark figure on the rooftop.

Located at 24 Avenida Menendez in St. Augustine.

The reports of ghostly happenings are so numerous in Florida that there are no less than three paranormal investigative teams to check them out. There's the North Florida Paranormal Research Inc., the Central Florida Paranormal Group, and the Daytona Beach Paranormal Research Group. These groups send teams to scientifically investigate and report on supernatural events throughout the state.

Cawthon Hall • Tallahassee

Florida State University's Cawthon Hall is said to be haunted by the ghost of a female student. It seems that in the 1940s, a young lady was sunbathing on a balcony of the dormitory, when a freak thunderstorm blew up. Although the sky over the dorm was blue, a sudden bolt of lightning streaked across the cloudless expanse, dodged a turret or two, and zapped the hapless swimsuited maiden, giving a whole new meaning to the term "frying your buns in the sun." Since that time, occupants of the girl's room report unexplained noises at night, objects being moved, and an overwhelming sense of otherworldly company.

Located on Dogwood Way on the FSU campus.

Dead Zone of I-4 • Seminole County

Drivers on I-4 beware! If your radio is suddenly overtaken with static, or if your cell phone won't work, you've just entered the Dead Zone! Better be careful: this short distance of about a quarter of a mile has witnessed more than its share of traffic accidents since about 1961. And here's why.

The strange history of this area began in 1887, when the Florida Land and Colonization Company tried to establish a Roman Catholic Colony in this area. The four or five immigrant families that settled in the area fell victim to yellow fever, and were buried without ceremony, since the priest who had settled with them had been called away to minister to other victims, and had succumbed to the epidemic himself.

Early in the 1900s, another attempt was made to settle the area, with due respect paid to the graves. The little community that sprang up set the small cemetery apart, and all was good and respectful. For a while. But the land was purchased by the state for the building of I-4. Instead of moving the graves, the state found it easier to cover them with dirt to elevate the new highway.

Those who know the story say that at the very time the dirt was dumped over the graves, Hurricane Donna crossed the state in an odd path. She was the worst storm to hit central Florida for a century. Coincidence? You decide. But since the opening of I-4, there has been an extremely high number of accidents right at the graves, reports confirmed by highway accident records. To add insult to injury, the state has refused to place a historical marker at the area, judging that the graves "are not historically significant."

The Dead Zone is located beneath the east-bound lane of I-4, at the south end of the bridge over the St. Johns River in Seminole County.

The Haunting of Florida

Devil's Chair • Cassadaga

Hey, wanna talk to the Devil? Well, in a cemetery in this small town is a grave, and next to the grave sits a bench. Legend has it that this is the devil's chair, and if you sit in it at midnight, the devil himself will appear. You can sit among the dead, many whose souls the old demon, no doubt, has claimed, and converse with the prince of darkness. Uh-huh.

Dorr House • Pensacola

The Dorr house was built by Clara Barkley Dorr, widow of lumber tycoon Eben Dorr, in 1871. Mrs. Dorr's ghost is

believed to be haunting the manor, and it seems she's a bit of a prude. It's said that when a woman wearing a short skirt stands in front of the floor-to-ceiling mirror in the house's formal sitting room, she will feel a tug at the hem of her skirt, as if someone is trying make it cover more. Many visitors have reported smelling a strong scent of fresh cut roses (Mrs.

The Dorr House in Pensacola is supposedly haunted by the ghost of Clara Dorr, a widow who had the house built in 1871.
Courtesy of the Pensacola Historical Society

Dorr's favorite flower), followed by extreme cold, and hearing soft crying sounds coming from an upstairs sewing room.

Located at 311 S. Adam Street.

FLORIDA SUNSHINE SKYWAY BRIDGE • ST. PETERSBURG

There have been numerous reports of the Florida Sunshine Skyway Bridge being frequented by a female ghost wearing tight jeans and a T-shirt. She hitches a ride on one end of the bridge, but by the time you reach the other end, she's disappeared!

Located south of St. Petersburg, the bridge spans Tampa Bay, connecting Pinellas and Manatee counties, and passing through Hillsborough County.

GRAY HOUSE • PENSACOLA

The Gray House on Alcaniz Street is said to be haunted by the ghost of a sea captain named Thomas Moristo, who lived there in the 1700s. Those who have lived in the house since

The Gray House on Alcaniz Street in Pensacola is said to be haunted by the ghost of a sea captain named Thomas Moristo, who lived there in the 1700s.
Courtesy of E.W. Bullock Associates

Moristo's death swear he's still there protecting the premises. In several incidents, residents have put food on the stove and left the room, returning moments later to find the stove has been turned off. A resident who was painting the home once left the paint and materials inside the home's foyer and retired for the evening. The next morning he arose and found all the paint and materials waiting for him—outside. There have been so many reports of apparitions of the old man rambling around in the home that many people are afraid to go inside.

HOLIDAY INN • PANAMA CITY BEACH

Guests staying in one of the rooms on the top floor of the Holiday Inn report seeing a headless man standing between the double beds. He's wearing a white T-shirt, with a pair of sunglasses hung around his neck. Of course, since he has no head, they are quite useless to him, we guess. He also seems to be a music critic because he keeps changing the radio station.

Located at 11127 West Highway 98 in Panama City Beach.

LITTLE RED ROCKER • SANFORD

This chair is about one hundred years old, and probably ranks among the oldest pieces of children's furniture in Florida. That's not so strange, but what is, is that it is said to rock on its own in the night. According to legend, the ghost of a deceased child still rocks in the chair. Researchers have documented two children who once used the chair, both of whom died before the age of ten in the 1920s. Could it be true? You decide when you see the chair at the Museum of Seminole County History, just off 17-92 in Sanford.

The Bermuda Triangle

Florida's most famous mystery is that of the Bermuda Triangle, a region of the Atlantic Ocean between Miami, Bermuda, and Puerto Rico. Within the triangle formed by these three points, many unexplained mysteries have occurred. Although there are no official records, it's believed that hundreds of boats and planes have vanished without a trace, and as many as one thousand people have lost their lives here. Even Columbus recorded in his ship's log that his compass was giving bizarre readings in the area. Japanese and Filipino seaman have long called the area Devil's Sea because of the strange occurrences here.

All sorts of reasons have been cited for these strange disappearances. Sea monsters and alien abductions are popular culprits. Some believe the area is the portal into another dimension, a Stargate, if you will, where all the disappeared are living the high life.

My favorite hypothesis is the ocean-poot theory. Yep, some scientists think that a sudden release of pent-up methane gas at the bottom of the ocean causes so much ocean and air turbulence that ships can sink and planes can crash without warning. Huh. Who knew old Neptune's flatulence could be so dangerous?

The Bermuda Triangle has been studied and debated for decades, but the mystery remains.

The Haunting of Florida

MIAMI RIVER INN • MIAMI

The Miami River Inn is one of Miami's most historic buildings. Built in 1910, it has slept many a U.S. president. The inn has been painstakingly restored and is a popular resort, but some guests get a bit more than they bargained for. Several guests have asked to be moved from one particular cabin because of repeating sounds throughout the night. They say that beginning around 11:00 p.m., there is the sound of a door opening and shutting, feet scraping on a mat, then after a brief silence, the sound of running toward the room and the shaking of the doorknob. Next, there's the sound of glass breaking outside the door, someone running up stairs, and then on the floor above, the sound and vibration of furniture being moved. Hard to get a good night's sleep with all that going on.

Visit this entry on the National Register of Historic Places at 118 SW South River Drive in Miami.

OLD JAIL • AMELIA ISLAND

The Old Jail on Amelia Island was the site of a particularly gory scene. Luc Simone Aury, bastard son of pirate Luis Aury, was a much-hated criminal, wanted for such heinous crimes as murder, rape, and robbery. When word of his capture spread, a large crowd of bloodthirsty citizens amassed to witness his execution. On the eve of his hanging, however, Aury managed to slit his own throat, hoping to deprive the good citizens of the humiliating display of his death. Jail authorities rustled up a surgeon to crudely baste him back together and keep him alive until they could kill him all over again the next day. With his collar buttoned to hide the wound, Aury was dragged to the gallows for his appointed hanging. When the trap was sprung, and Aury dropped, the rope all but decapitated him, and blood spewed over the crowd. Pandemonium ensued, with women fainting and children crying.

Today, there are reports that Aury can be heard moaning in the vicinity of the old gallows, and on occasion, his ghost will appear, with the blood-soaked gash visible across his neck.

You can reach Amelia Island by using exit 129 off I-95.

PENSACOLA LIGHTHOUSE • PENSACOLA

Since most lighthouses have a ghost or two, and this lighthouse in particular is the oldest one on the Gulf Coast, it's not surprising that it's said to be haunted by its first keeper, Jeremiah Ingram. Many report feeling cold spots when entering and touring it, footsteps are heard coming down the tower stairs, and doors open and close by themselves. Come tour Jeremiah's quarters, and enjoy historical exhibits.

Located at the Pensacola Naval Air Station at the entrance to Pensacola Bay.

The Pensacola Lighthouse is believed to be haunted by a former keeper.
Courtesy of E.W. Bullock Associates

The Haunting of Florida

SPANISH MILITARY HOSPITAL • ST. AUGUSTINE

The Spanish Military Hospital is a bona fide haunted building, featured, no less, on the Travel Channel's *Liars and Legends* show. The hospital was investigated by North Florida Paranormal Research, Inc., which found the place to be one of the most active (paranormally) places they've ever investigated. The group photographed anomalies and videotaped objects being thrown by unseen hands. There were strange cold spots, confirmed by thermometers, and some unseen entity unplugged the power cord to the video camera. And don't forget about the doors that open and close by themselves! Some people say it's because the hospital was built on ground used for Spanish and Indian burials. At any rate, inhabitants of the building and the ghosts don't bother each other, and they peacefully co-exist at 3 Aviles Street in St. Augustine.

ST. PAUL'S CEMETERY • KEY WEST

St. Paul's Cemetery is a favorite haunt in Key West. It's the burial spot of Commander Thomas Randolph, a soldier who was sent to Key West to rid the place of pirates and smugglers. He was very good at his job and is a bit of a hero here. Reports are that his spirit can be seen wandering the cemetery at night.

TAMPA THEATER • TAMPA

The Tampa Theater is believed to be haunted by the ghost of a young man who worked there in the 1940s. The man loved his job and worked there until his death. Today, employees report hearing footsteps and chains in deserted hallways. There have also been reports of drafts of icy air and a feeling of being grabbed by the neck.

Come see a film or enjoy a concert at this landmark on Franklin Street.

Lobby of the Tampa Theater, reported to be haunted
by the ghost of a former employee.
Courtesy of the Tampa Bay Convention & Visitors Bureau

Funny Festivals and Such

Motorcycle mamas, rattlesnake celebrations, revelers in the streets, seafood going crazy. ... There's just no end to the funny goings-on in Strange But True Florida.

CHUMUCKLA REDNECK PARADE • CHUMUCKLA

The Chumuckla Redneck Parade is a joke. Well, at least it was a joke when it first started about twelve years ago. Seems a bunch of good ole boys got a bit inebriated one Christmas Eve and had to be paraded home by their long-suffering wives. They jokingly repeated the parade the next year, and things just grew from there.

Today, as many as fifteen thousand people come to watch the parade, which has grown into a two-day festival and has gained national attention.

True to Florida festival form, the celebration includes the election of a Redneck King and Queen, who appear in all their finery, which for the Queen might include a prom dress, a spackling of makeup, beehive hairdo, and a set of Bubba teeth—you know, the ones that look like they come right out of *Deliverance*. There's also a beauty pageant to choose the year's Miss Fish Camp America.

In the parade, there're rednecks driving all manner of vehicles—motorcycles, tractors, and of course, pick-up trucks. There's plenty of food and drink to be had. Music and dancing.

Funny Festivals and Such

Clowns. Arts and crafts. And Bubba teeth. Lots and lots of Bubba teeth.

Proceeds from the festival go to benefit Chumuckla's needy children at Christmas.

Held the second weekend in December.

DAYTONA BEACH BIKE WEEK • DAYTONA BEACH

Maybe you haven't noticed, but motorcycling has become the pastime of millions of ordinary people. Doctors and lawyers. Firefighters and steel workers. Even freelance writers. All have found that life is more fun when you're barreling through it astride 750 pounds of steel. (Mine's a Harley-Davidson Road King.)

Florida has two motorcycle rallies. The first and

Daytona Bike Week has been a tradition since 1937. Today, hundreds of thousands of visitors come to participate in the ten days of festivities every fall.
Courtesy of Daytona Beach Area Convention & Visitors Bureau Inc.

biggest is the Daytona Beach Bike Week. It began in 1937 and has grown into a ten-day mega-event, attended by hundreds of thousands of bikers on their thundering steel steeds.

It's Motorcycle Mecca. There's motorcycle racing, (sorta)

organized rides, drinking, and partying. It's a pretty wild week, both for the bikers and those who happen to be visiting Daytona Beach.

Bike Week is held the second weekend in March.

FANTASMAL FESTIVAL FUN • KEY WEST

There's a really fun festival that happens in Key West every October. It's wild and crazy. Wilder and crazier even than that little festival they have every February in New Orleans. And we want to tell you all about it. There's just one problem.

The Key West Tourism Development Association has trademarked the name of this wild and crazy festival, so we can't name it for you without getting written permission. Imagine! Having to get permission for anything in Key West! It's a travesty!

Wild and colorful costumes are part of this Key West celebration held each October.
Courtesy of the Florida Keys and Key West Monroe County Tourist Development Council

Anyway, what we'll have to do is give you the details about this fantasy of a festival. We just won't name it for you.

The phantasmagoric festivities begin ten days before Halloween and culminate in a phreaky phrenzy on that night of phright. (Sorry. I'll stop) There're toga parties! Masquerade balls! A pet masquerade parade! A pimp and ho costume contest! A drunken promenade down Duval Street! A royal coronation ball for the crowning of the festival king and queen! Come as you aren't parties!

You can revel in the streets every night for ten nights straight. Get scared by Key West ghosts on the many ghost tours (not to mention the fright you'll get at the sight of some of your fellow revelers!). Dress up like the monster you are for the Monster's Ball. Or shed your clothes and get your costume painted on. Tickle your fantasy and heat up your libido at the Feathers and Fantasy masquerade ball, advertised for the lusty and the luscious. Join the "girls" and "boys" at 801 Bourbon Street Bar for a leather fetish party that's not for the shy. Indulge in "hot screams and wet dreams" with the drag queens at a poolside party. And that's just a mere sampling of the partying going on and the sights that you'll see.

In case you haven't figured it out, this phantasy party is for adults only. So prepare yourself. Although dancing in the streets is illegal and is frowned upon by the Key West Tourism Development Association, don't be surprised to see nude bodies, some covered in body paint, some not, sashaying past you. And should you lose all inhibitions and decide you'd like to grin and bare it as well, just remember … dancing in the streets is illegal and is frowned upon by the Key West Tourism Development Association. So keep a look out for the phantasy police.

The wild and crazy party culminates with a golden, glittering parade hosted by Captain Morgan (who else?), featuring outrageous floats, dazzling marching bands, and outlandish dancing groups. Come early, though, for there'll be roughly seventy thousand bleary-eyed revelers there to see it.

Well, that about sums it up, and looks like we did it. We told you all about that festival fantasy down in Key West without violating even one trademark law. So, there! PFFT!

FESTIVALS OF THE SEA COW • ORANGE CITY/CRYSTAL RIVER

As the official state marine mammal, the manatee is celebrated throughout Florida. Once plentiful along the coastal waters, this so-ugly-it's-cute sea cow is now at the point of extinction and has for many years been the object of fundraising and consciousness-raising drives in an effort to save the species.

That's the goal of Florida's two manatee festivals. At the Blue Springs Manatee Festival in Orange City, you can learn about the manatee and, if you're lucky, observe a few of them in their own environment—Blue Springs. There's also dancing and music, food, arts and crafts, endangered wildlife exhibitions, and children's activities. Held in late January.

It's pretty much the same at the Florida Manatee Festival in Crystal River, except for the boat tours. At this festival, you can take a sightseeing boat tour in search of the nearly two hundred manatees that winter in Crystal River. Held in early January.

FLORIDA SEAFOOD FESTIVAL • APALACHICOLA

Yum! Check out the Florida Seafood Festival, held annually in Apalachicola's Battery Park. Florida's oldest maritime exhibit, the three-day event features lots of good seafood and plenty of fun.

If you really, really like oysters, you can try your hand, er, stomach at the oyster-eating contest. But you really, really gotta like the slimy little boogers because here it's nothing but oysters. No crackers. No sauce. Just oyster after slimy oyster. The one who eats the most wins, and the only requirement is that they stay down. Some of the really serious contestants have been known to consume as many as three hundred oysters.

Every November, the three-day seafood festival is held at Apalachicola's Battery Park. Oyster eating and shucking events are some of the highlights.
Courtesy of Dana Whaley

Before the oyster-eating contest, there's an oyster shucking contest, one of the fastest events you'll witness. Each contestant has a tray with eighteen Apalachicola oysters in front of them. When the whistle blows, there's a blur of activity, and often within two minutes, a contestant signals that he's finished. But he's not necessarily the winner. The competition continues until all the oysters have been shucked. Judges then examine each oyster, and they are serious about their oysters in Apalachicola. Any contestant that mutilates an oyster is disqualified. Penalty time is added for nicks, loose shell, or other dastardly deeds.

Manatee Facts

1. Manatees belong to the order *Sirenia*. The word sirenia is derived from the word siren, the legendary Greek sea beauties that lured sailors to their deaths with their singing. Many believe that early mermaid sightings were actually manatee sightings.

2. An adult manatee can weigh up to 1,200 pounds and measure up to twelve feet long.

3. Manatees eat about 15 percent of their body weight daily.

4. Manatees have no natural enemies. They can live sixty years or more, but because of human-related fatalities, such as run-ins with boats, ingestion of fish hooks, plastic, and other pollution, and loss of habitat, they are on the endangered species list.

5. The manatee has just one calf every two to five years.

6. The manatee is protected under the federal Marine Mammal Protection Act, which makes it illegal to harass, hunt, capture, or kill any marine mammal. It's also protected by the Florida Manatee Sanctuary Act, which makes it illegal to intentionally or negligently annoy, molest, harass, or disturb any manatee.

7. Anyone violating the state law could face a maximum fee of $1,000 and/or sixty days imprisonment. Anyone violating the federal law faces a maximum $100,000 fine and/or one year in prison.

Funny Festivals and Such

The festival also features arts and crafts exhibits, live entertainment, a parade, and a five-kilometer run. And don't miss the Blessing of the Fleet, where local clergymen bless the colorful parade of fishing, shrimping, and oystering vessels—and any other boat that happens by.

Held annually in November.

Gasparilla Pirate Fest • Tampa Bay

There are buccaneers in Tampa Bay, and we're not talking football. We're talking about the legendary Jose Gaspar, who terrorized the western coastal waters of Florida during the eighteen century. But by 1821, he was tired of the pirate's life. All that swash and buckling was getting to him, we suppose.

Anyway, as the story goes, Gaspar had just convinced his band of merry brigands to give it all up, to disband, take their ill-gotten gains, and retire to Florida. But wait! What's that on the horizon? A merchant ship, laden, no doubt, with gold and jewels. Whaddya say, Cap'n? Just one more little ship? Just a bit more treasure to add to the retirement fund?

Costumed pirates aboard the *Jose Gasparilla* wave their pistols at the crowds gathered for Tampa's annual Gasparilla Pirate Fest.
Courtesy of EventMakers Corporation, Tampa

Gaspar and his band attacked the merchant ship, expecting a quick overthrow. To their surprise, they found themselves in a bloody battle. Turns out the merchant ship was really the *U.S.S. Enterprise*, a U.S. Navy warship, in disguise. Gaspar, who often called himself Gasparilla, and his men fought a fierce battle, but they were no match for the U.S. Navy. According to legend, as the commanding officer of the *Enterprise* stepped aboard the defeated ship, Gaspar wrapped the anchor chain around his waist, and with his sword brandished in defiance, he leapt overboard. He reportedly left a pirate's fortune buried somewhere along the Florida coast.

The story of Gaspar was revived in 1904, when civic leaders in Tampa were planning a city festival. As a unique part of the celebration, the leaders formed the secret Ye Mystic Krewe of Gasparilla, a group of forty leaders who, masked and costumed in pirate garb, surprised the city with a mock pirate attack. Because they lacked sea transportation, this krewe arrived on horseback and "captured the city" during the festival parade. And so was born the Gasparilla Pirate Fest.

In 1954, Ye Mystic Krewe of Gasparilla commissioned the building of the *Jose Gasparilla*, the world's only modern-day, fully-rigged pirate ship. A replica of an eighteenth-century West Indiaman, the ship is 165-feet long, with three 100-foot steel masts.

During the second week of February, the Gasparilla Pirate Fest commences with a full week of activities, culminating with the capture of Tampa on Saturday. The ship enters Tampa Bay, intent on invasion. There's a brief skirmish with a defending flotilla, but the flotilla is no match for Gaspar and his pirates.

Funny Festivals and Such

The ship sails into port and seizes the city. A parade ensues. So does partying. And fireworks. In fact, a good time is had by all. And, hey, nobody's trademarked the name, so we can say it out loud without written permission. It's the GASPARILLA PIRATE FEST in Tampa. Don't miss it.

King Mango Strut • Coconut Grove

If you were to tell the participants in Coconut Grove's annual King Mango Strut that they were acting in poor taste, they'd likely say "thank you." In fact, poor taste is the abiding theme of this zany parade, and the more tasteless the better.

The parade is political satire on wheels. Anything featured in the news during the year is fair game. In the 2004 parade, there was Martha Stewart demonstrating how to decorate small spaces, Scott Peterson declaring his innocence from a rolling electric chair, Cialis users who were "suffering" that four-hour thingy you keep marveling over, Floridians suffering premature evacuation, contraceptive Sponge Bob, and the lady who found Osama bin Laden for President Bush. You get the picture.

The parade is a parody of the Orange Bowl's King Orange Jamboree parade. It began in 1982, when a group of marchers playing "unsuitable" instruments, such as kazoos, was denied permission to march in that hallowed parade. Every year, a hilarious take-off of the King Orange Jamboree parade is included in the King Mango Strut.

It's lots of crazy fun. So, if you're in Florida and it's the weekend before New Year's, hop on over to Coconut Grove. Just remember to leave your good taste at home.

RATTLESNAKE FESTIVAL • SAN ANTONIO

Yep, that's what we said. A Rattlesnake Festival. For almost forty years, the good folks of San Antonio (yes, Florida) have been celebrating rattlesnakes. In the beginning they would coax the toothsome creatures from their dark holes in an annual roundup and award prizes for the biggest one found.

Today, the festival is a celebration of the rattlesnake, with educational reptile shows, music, food, and arts and crafts shows. There's also a five-kilometer Rattlesnake Run. (No, silly, that's for humans. Snakes can't run. No legs.) But hey! Don't miss those turtle races!

This is just one of the many slithering specimens at San Antonio's Rattlesnake Festival.
Courtesy of Wild Florida Productions of Miami

Held annually on the third Saturday in October.

THUNDER ON THE BEACH • PANAMA CITY

Florida's other bike rally, Thunder on the Beach, is held in Panama City. It's much smaller—with thousands of bikers instead of hundreds of thousands—but the concept is the same: ride, party, ride, eat, party, ride. For those of us who don't like big crowds, this is the place to be.

Thunder on the Beach occurs the last weekend in April.

Funny Festivals and Such

UMATILLA BEAR FESTIVAL • UMATILLA

Bears! When you think of Florida, you don't usually think of bears. With all the dolphins, manatees, and flamingos around, the Florida black bear is pretty much a nonentity. Except in Umatilla. This little town near Orlando is located at the mouth of the Ocala National Forest, the last stronghold of central Florida's endangered black bear.

The purpose of the festival is to educate people on the black bears and their plight in Florida—where almost twenty acres of wildlife habitat is lost every hour. There are educational presentations with notable wildlife personalities such as Jim Fowler, three-hour field trips into the Ocala National Forest, and a five-kilometer run.

Christopher Columbus reported seeing mermaids in his travels around the Caribbean. He must not have been near Weeki Wachee, though, for he reported that these mermaids were not as beautiful as he had heard.

I reckon not. Old Chris's mermaids were cows, literally. Historians believe that Chris and other sailors who reported mermaid sightings were actually seeing manatees, also called sea cows. Possibly the unique rounded shape of the manatee's tail looked enough like a mermaid's tail to fool the sailors. Maybe. But what about those whiskers? No doubt those guys had been at sea way too long!

Eat, Drink, And Be Merry!

Eating Out

Eating out in Strange But True Florida is more than a meal. It's an experience. You can dine with pirates. Drink with gangsters. Heck, you can even dance naked!

ALLIGATOR ALLEY NATIVE FLORIDA RESTAURANT AND MUSIC HALL • FORT LAUDERDALE

This place offers down-home Southern cuisine with a Florida flair. Their gumbo is award-winning, and the barbecued gator ribs (a rare treat!) have been featured on cable television's Food Network. There's also gator scallopini, buffalo gator, and fried gator bites.

There's live music nightly featuring both national and local artists performing a variety of music styles—blues, jazz, rock, punk, and funk.

Located at 1321 East Commercial Boulevard in Oakland Park.

ANGEL'S DINER • PALATKA

Longing for the good old days? You know the ones, when Coca-Cola was a nickel and hamburgers didn't come with special sauce? For a step back to those days, you can't beat Angel's Diner. Opened in 1932, Angel's is Florida's oldest diner, and it still offers mouthwatering diner fare—to-die-for cheeseburgers, fried onion rings, and thick, creamy shakes.

Fashioned from an old railroad dining car, the décor is 1950s neon kitschy. There's curb service and a jukebox filled with nostalgic classics. But get there early. The place is small, and it fills up fast.

Located at 209 Reid Street.

BARNACLE BILL'S • ST. AUGUSTINE

How could you pass up a place called Barnacle Bill's? You can't. You won't go wrong, either, because in addition to its picturesque name, Barnacle Bill's has good food. The locals eat here, and it's consistently voted the most referred restaurant by St. Augustine's hotel and resort staff.

While you're there, be sure to pick up a bottle of Dat'l Do-It sauce made from St. Augustine's famous datil peppers. But don't forget to pay for it! Owner Chris Way concocted the sauce twenty years ago when the restaurant first opened. He noticed that bottles of the sauce kept disappearing, leaving secreted in the pockets and purses of his guests. He figured that if they'd steal it, maybe they'd buy it, so he began bottling the sauce and selling it in the restaurant.

There are now two Barnacle Bill's. The original restaurant is located at 14 Castillo Drive in the historic district. The new addition is located at 451 A1A Beach Boulevard.

BOSS OYSTER • APALACHICOLA

This little-known town on the east Panhandle coast is known as the Oyster Capital of Florida, with good reason. Franklin County, where Apalachicola is located, produces 90 percent of Florida's oysters and 10 percent of the country's.

So it stands to reason that Boss Oyster is the place to get the plumpest, sweetest raw oysters. Right? Exactly. In fact, until Papa Joe's opened down the road a couple of years ago, the renovated cotton warehouse was the only place in town to get oysters.

And they're served just as they should be … with beer and hot sauce and a roll of paper towels.

You can get other seafood at Boss Oyster as well. But why? As that wise troubadour Jimmy Buffet says, "Give me oysters and beer/ Every day of the year/ And I'll be fine/I'll feel fi-i-i-ne."

Located at 123 Water Street.

CABBAGE KEY INN AND RESTAURANT • CABBAGE KEY

Looking for a cheeseburger in paradise? Come to the Cabbage Key Inn and Restaurant. Rumor has it that this restaurant was the inspiration for Jimmy Buffet's song "Cheeseburger In Paradise." Getting there is a little difficult, since Cabbage Key is accessible only by boat, well, and helicopter or seaplane. If you don't have a boat, you can catch a ferry cruise out from Pine Island.

Once you make it there, you might not want to leave. This is Florida as she used to be. No cars. No paved highways. No mouse ears. Just one hundred acres of tropical paradise.

Built in the 1930s by the family of novelist Mary Roberts Rinehart, the historic Cabbage Key Inn and Restaurant sits atop a 38-foot Indian shell mound, surrounded by nature trails and all manner of wildlife. Activities here tend toward relaxation: Shelling on nearby beaches, reading, writing, boating, nature walks, etc.

Eat, Drink, And Be Merry!

Meals in the restaurant are prepared from ingredients boated over daily. The menu includes such interesting items as seafood strudel and grouper tortuga. And cheeseburgers in paradise. The gleaming wood paneling is decorated by shelves of books, antique fishing lures, pictures, and trophy fish.

The Dollar Bill Bar, located within the restaurant, gets its name from the thousands of dollar bills that are taped across the ceiling and walls of the bar. This unique décor comes from an old tradition among the early fishermen of the island, who would leave a signed dollar bill taped to the wall, so they'd at least have that much if their day of fishing was unprofitable.

You're invited to leave one taped there yourself—and when you return for another visit someday, you can then search out your lost dollar. There are more than fifty thousand bills taped there. Those that fall, the proprietor says, are collected and donated to charity.

Despite its remoteness, the restaurant and bar do a brisk business, thanks to the boaters from many ports who stop in. You're as likely to share a meal or a drink with a celebrity as with a local here. Who knows? Maybe Mr. Buffet will return for more inspiration!

Located in the Intercoastal Waterway at marker #60.

CAPONE'S DINNER & SHOW • KISSIMMEE

Back in the 1930s, things weren't always as they seemed. The government was in the midst of its little social experiment—Prohibition—and behind the doors of something as innocent-looking as an ice cream parlor, the law was being broken. At Capone's Dinner & Show you can take a step back to those days, when there was a speakeasy around every corner, and the mob ruled. The evening begins innocently enough. Youse buys your ticket and gets your instructions. Knock three times on the secret door, and give Vinnie the password. Get it right, or youse won't get in.

Once inside, help yourself to the all-you-can-eat buffet (Italian, of course!), and Babyface'll bring youse some hootch. Unlimited draft

Visitors to the Capone's Dinner Show in Kissimmee enjoy a musical comedy show set in the 1930s and an all-you-can-eat buffet.
Courtesy of Capone's Dinner & Show

beer, sangria, Al's special rumrunners, and soft drinks are included. There's a cash bar if youse wants something stronger.

Enjoy the show (an original musical revue), and youse can dance later. Have fun, and remember, when you leave, don't be singing to no coppers!

Sorry 'bout that. Couldn't resist.

Located at 4740 West Highway 192.

Eat, Drink, And Be Merry!

CAPTAIN MEMO'S ORIGINAL PIRATE CRUISE • CLEARWATER

Pirates who are hankering to actually take to the high seas can hop aboard the Pirate's Ransom for a cruise around Clearwater Beach on Captain Memo's Original Pirate Cruise. Captain Memo, who gained his pirate experience as an insurance salesman in a former life; first mate, wife Panama Pam; and their raggedy band of brigands will shanghai you and force you to eat, drink, and be merry. There's dolphin watching, treasure hunting, dancing, water games, and face painting. Hoist the Jolly Roger and belly up to the bar with such skilled seamen as Blackjack Jerry, Diamond Diane, Dastardly Dan, and Gangplank Gary.

Located at Clearwater Marina.

THE CRAB SHACK • ST. PETERSBURG

The Crab Shack is the classic Florida seafood shanty. Housed in a shabby, authentic-looking fisherman's shack, the restaurant advertises a casual, no-frills dining experience. The menu is impressive, with twenty-seven different items on the appetizer menu alone. There's all kinds of broiled, steamed, fried, smoked, and blackened seafood (blue crab is the specialty), stews and soups, sandwiches, pasta, salads, and desserts. There's also a Little Skipper's menu for the young 'uns.

Located at 11400 Gandy Boulevard.

DAVE AND BUSTER'S • JACKSONVILLE

Always envied the kids in places like Chuckie Cheese, where playing is as important as eating? Well, envy no more, because now the grownups have their own play and eat restaurant. Dave and Buster's has basketball, billiards, a home run derby, and shuffleboard. And that's just the tame stuff. There are also video games and virtual simulator games, such as *Star Trek Voyager*, *Star Wars Trilogy*, *Ferrari F355 Challenge*, and *Airline Pilot*, where you can challenge each other.

There is, of course, also a restaurant and two bars: the Viewpoint, where you can sit and watch all the action, and the Midway, which is where the action is.

Located at 7025 Salisbury Road.

FLORA-BAMA LOUNGE • PENSACOLA

The Flora-Bama Lounge straddles the Florida/ Alabama state line, and so you'll find it also featured in our *Strange But True Alabama*, where it's billed as possibly the state's most famous—and craziest—bar. Considering some of Florida's Key West entries, we can't make that claim here. It is, however, the most fun you'll have in the northern latitudes.

Opened in 1961 as a hole-in-the-wall dive, the Flora-Bama has grown into the quintessential beach bar. It's perched precariously on the sparkling blue Gulf and has everything for the discerning reveler: three band stages, ten bars, an oyster bar, a large fenced-in party area, beach volleyball courts, a package store, and even a recording studio. On September 16, 2004, Hurricane Ivan demolished the Flora-Bama, but plans were soon underway to bring it back to its glory.

It's not just the accommodations that make the Flora-Bama so popular, though. There's a laid-back, beach attitude that permeates the atmosphere and spurs a multitude of strange goings-on. Consider if you will:

The Polar Bear Dip in the Gulf. January 1, 2005, marked the twentieth anniversary of this strange ritual. Crazy people gather at the Flora-Bama, strip to their swimsuits or maybe even their birthday suits, and take a plunge into the frigid Gulf.

The Easter Bunny Drop and Egg Hunt, where the Easter Bunny parachutes down to the bar and hides more than three thousand of his little eggs up and down the beach for partygoers to find.

The Mullet Man Triathlon, with categories such as the Athena for women 145 pounds or more, the Clydesdale and Super Clydesdale for men 200 pounds or more, and the Fat Tire for men and women riding fat tire vehicles or bicycles.

The Interstate Mullet Toss. Held annually on the last Friday in April, this competition draws hundreds of competitors from Alabama and Florida to see who can throw a dead mullet the farthest distance over the Alabama state line. Thousands of partyers come from around the country to watch.

The Miss Firecracker Bikini Contest. OK, that one is pretty much expected of a beach bar.

Located at 17401 Perdido Key Drive.

FOX'S SHERRON INN • MIAMI

Stepping into Fox's Sherron Inn is like taking a step back in time—1946 to be exact. That's the year Fox's opened, and not much has changed since. The lighting is still dim. The patrons still sit in the original red vinyl booths. And you can still find

Frank Sinatra on the jukebox. Of course, you can also find Britney Spears, but nothing's perfect.

The drinks are made the old-fashioned way, good and stiff, and the food is a notch up from typical dive bar fare in this throwback restaurant-lounge. Liver and onions, fried clams, frog legs in garlic butter, and New York strip are just a sample of what you'll find.

Located at 6030 South Dixie Highway.

GATOR'S CAFÉ AND SALOON • TREASURE ISLAND

Gator's Café and Saloon claims to have the world's longest waterfront bar. The food is typical Florida beach fare—hot dogs, smoked fish sandwiches, and barbecue, with plenty of frozen drinks to wash it all down.

The place is also a sports bar—well, football, anyway. The owners are obviously University of Florida fans, and the place is filled with Gators memorabilia.

Located at 12754 Kingfish Drive.

MACDINTON'S IRISH PUB & RESTAURANT • TAMPA

Hankering for a wee bit o' the Irish? Stop in at MacDinton's Irish Pub & Restaurant for a pint of Guinness served up with a bit of Irish blarney. The establishment's owners are all Irish emigrants, so you can be sure the brogues you hear are real and the feel of the old country is authentic.

Menu items include shepherd's pie, Irish smoked salmon, corned beef and cabbage, and Irish stew. A bit o' the Emerald Isle on the Emerald Coast, eh?

Located at 405 South Howard Avenue.

Eat, Drink, And Be Merry!

TREASURE SHIP RESTAURANT • PANAMA CITY

Ahoy there, matey! Step aboard the Treasure Ship Restaurant and get lost in another time. The restaurant/shopping complex is housed within a 200-foot replica of a seventeenth-century Spanish galleon. Galleons are known as treasure ships because they not only looted the New World of its riches, but they also were often captured and used by pirates to steal away those ill-gotten gains from the Spanish.

You can indulge your pirate fantasies here. Enjoy food with a Caribbean flare in the Hook's Grill and Grog (legend has it this

was Captain Hook's favorite food), located on the deck level. The ship's main dining area, on the second level, features standard surf and turf fare, but it's Captain Crabby's on the third level that will get the kids' vote as the place to dine. Billed as "a bountiful all-you-can-eat adventure with excitement and pirate lore,"

The Treasure Ship Restaurant is housed within a replica of a seventeenth century Spanish galleon. Courtesy of Panama City Beach Convention & Visitors Bureau

the restaurant promises live entertainment with the blast of cannons and real pirates offering balloon animals and face-painting right at the table.

There's also a video arcade, The Pirate's Playroom, to keep the little swashbucklers occupied while mom and dad relax with a bit o' the grog deckside. And don't forget to stop by the gift shop for a few souvenir treasures to take home.

Located at 3605 Thomas Drive.

WHITEY'S FISH CAMP • ORANGE PARK

Whitey's Fish Camp opened in 1963 as your run-of-the-mill fishing camp, offering camping and bait and tackle. In 1969, proprietors Whitey and Ann Ham added a restaurant, concentrating on serving up the catfish caught in the area.

Whitey's Fish Camp has been a haven for seafood lovers since 1969, with its fried catfish and fried swamp vittles.
Courtesy of Whitey's Fish Camp

Both the camp and the restaurant have evolved through the years. Today, the restaurant is a full-fledged sports bar large enough to accommodate three hundred people. The specialty is still fried catfish (still locally caught), but the menu has expanded to include an array of seafood choices. The most interesting items are the fried swamp vittles, which include gator tail, turtle, frog legs, and soft shell crab.

Located at 2032 County Road 220.

World Class Partying

Pub crawling is a world-class event. But it ain't for amateurs. Even elite drinking athletes, such as Papa Hemingway and Jimmy Buffet, have found themselves floored here. You gotta train before you go.

Eat, Drink, And Be Merry!

Pick a few of your funkiest local bars, the funkier the better. You know the kind. Lighting so dim you need a cane to find the bar. A few rickety tables scattered about. The bartenders are as bleary-eyed as the clientele. And all the art is on the bathroom walls.

Start out slow, a few beers as you travel from bar to bar. Move up to the hard stuff, stumbling as you go. In no time you'll be in prime pub-crawling condition: on your knees, shooting tequila.

Papa would be proud.

BLUE ANCHOR BRITISH PUB • DELRAY BEACH

If you're hankering for a bit of fish 'n' chips or a spot of tea on your tour of Florida, here's just the place for you. Here you'll find authentic British favorites in an atmosphere that'll make you think you're in foggy London Town. And there's a reason for that. The pub was actually shipped

The Blue Anchor was shipped from London, England, where it stood for 150 years in London's historic Chancery Lane.
Courtesy of the Delray Beach Chamber of Commerce

from England, brick by brick, where it stood for 150 years as the Blue Anchor Pub in London's historic Chancery Lane. Yep, the whole outside of the original pub—oak doors, paneling, and stained glass windows—was dismantled in sections and reassembled in Delray Beach to become the landmark that it is today on Atlantic Avenue.

Besides its British fare, the pub brings history with it as well. In its previous London life, it regularly welcomed the likes of Winston Churchill and Cardinal Thomas Wolsey, Henry VIII's Prime Minister. It also saw commoners like Elizabeth Stride and Catherine Eddows, two of Jack the Ripper's victims who were said to have spent their last night alive drinking at the Blue Anchor, and in the company of a strange man, no less.

With that dubious distinction, it probably won't surprise you to know that there are ghost stories attached to the place as well. Ask about those while you wet your whistle.

Located at 804 E. Atlantic Avenue in Delray Beach.

CABARET • KEY WEST

If you really want a walk on the wild side, you can't miss the Cabaret at the 801 Bourbon Street Bar. And don't get confused. We haven't traveled on little fairy feet to New Orleans; this Bourbon Street Bar is actually on Duval Street.

The Cabaret, located upstairs at the 801 Bourbon Street Bar complex, features musical shows nightly, headlined by famed performers, such as Sushi, RV Beaumont, and Scabola. And their names aren't all that are different about these "girls." Take a closer look. Is that a five o'clock shadow? Maybe. But it doesn't take away from the entertainment. The 801 Cabaret girls put on a fun show. Just don't be surprised to find yourself up there on stage with them.

Located at 801 Duval Street.

CAPTAIN TONY'S SALOON • KEY WEST

Captain Tony Terracino is a Key West legend. Jimmy Buffet said so in his song "Last Mango In Paris." So is his bar, Captain Tony's Saloon.

A former gunrunner and Key West mayor, Captain Tony opened the bar with friend "Sloppy Joe" Russell in 1933 in the old town morgue. The bar was the original Sloppy Joe's until a dispute over a $1-a-week rent increase angered Russell.

Legend has it that on one drunken night in 1937, Russell, with the help of faithful patron Papa

The legendary Captain Tony's Saloon in Key West boasts of being Florida's oldest bar and a favorite of the adventurous. Courtesy of Kevin Henderson

Hemingway and a few other drunks, picked up everything and moved the bar around the corner to Duval Street.

Dark and dank, Captain Tony's is the antithesis of the fancy tourist bar. The first thing you're likely to notice is the tree growing right there in the middle. Next, as you crawl in looking for your next shooter, you'll have to crawl over the tombstone. If you're not too bleary-eyed, you'll see that it reads "Reba

Sawyer 1900-1950."

Seems after her death, Reba's husband learned from love letters he discovered that she was having an affair. Reba and her paramour would meet at Captain Tony's. Angry, Reba's husband loaded her tombstone into the back of his pickup and threw it out in the street in front of the bar. He was heard to shout that if she wanted to be there so much, she could just spend eternity there. When Captain Tony learned that her family didn't want the tombstone back, he had it installed into the floor of the bar. True? Who knows? But it makes a good story, and that's all that counts.

Once you've recovered enough to haul yourself up to a barstool, take a look around. There are bras hanging everywhere. And car tags. And business cards. The quintessential dive décor. Oh, and look a little closer at the old man in the corner. Might just be Captain Tony. Now in his 80s, the old legend is a frequent visitor.

There's live music. Cold beer. Good company. What else is there?

Located at 328 Greene Street.

THE GARDEN OF EDEN • KEY WEST

Dance naked! The Garden of Eden is Key West's only clothing-optional bar. Located on the roof of the Bull and Whistle, an open-air bar on Duval Street, the Garden of Eden opens daily at 10:00 a.m. Patrons are invited to work on their all-over tans while quenching their thirst with tasty tropical drinks.

And when it's time to freshen up for the evening, no need

to leave. Just take a shower there and join everyone for the Naked Sunset celebration. There's live music at 5:00 p.m. and a DJ spinning records from 9:00 p.m. until 2:30 a.m. Dance the night away in the altogether!

Located on the corner of Caroline and Duval streets.

THE GREEN PARROT • KEY WEST

The motto here is: No snivelling [sic] since 1890.

Advertised as the first and last bar on U.S. 1, the Green Parrot is an open-air tropical saloon, with friendly (and bleary-eyed) bartenders and bad art hanging on the walls. The atmosphere is laid-back, the cocktails are "spine-tingling," and the clientele are "engagingly louche." (We looked it up. It means bleary-eyed. And disreputable.) You should fit right in.

The Green Parrot is mentioned in many a gritty mystery novel set in Key West, so as a fan of that genre, I knew of the bar long before I ever made it to Margaritaville. Surprisingly, it's also received praise in slick, upscale travel publications, such as *Travel & Leisure* and *Islands*. In 2000, the Green Parrot was even voted as one of the twenty-four best bars in the U.S. by *Playboy* magazine, a ringing endorsement if we ever heard one! It's a great place to start your pub crawl.

Located on the corner of Southard and Whitehead Streets.

McGUIRE'S IRISH PUB AND BREWERY • PENSACOLA AND DESTIN

The Blue Anchor is not the only pub that offers an international flair! For something Irish, try McGuire's.

This place is huge, and its maze of rooms will keep you entertained as you see the firefighters' room, the Notre Dame room, and an Irish aviator's room, just to name a few. A dominant theme is the life of McGuire's legendary Cousin Nathan, whose adventures are celebrated throughout the place. Apparently he did it all: he hobnobbed with celebrities, as signed photographs prove, and was an

It's tradition for first-time visitors to kiss the giant moose head in the main room of McGuire's Irish Pub and Brewery.
Courtesy of E.W. Bullock Associates

expert marksman, if the heads filling the walls are any sign. And you might as well know before you go, it's tradition for newcomers to kiss the giant moose head in the main room.

If that's not enough, you'll see more than $250,000 in one dollar bills hanging from the ceiling throughout the place, each one signed by "Irishmen of all nationalities." It seems that when the pub first opened in 1977, Molly the waitress tacked her first tip—one dollar—to the back bar for good luck. Friends who came to the pub added to it, and a tradition was born.

If you're in the mood to do more than drink, you can sample traditional Irish staples such as corned beef and cabbage and Irish stew. The Senate Bean Soup will satisfy the budget-conscious in more ways than one: it costs only 18 cents, still a bargain even though you're required to order another food item to go with it. By the way, it's made from the same recipe as the bean soup served in the U.S. Senate dining room.

And talk about the luck of the Irish! You can enjoy this Florida attraction in two locations: in Pensacola, you'll find McGuire's at 600 E. Gregory St., and in Destin, it's at 33 Highway 98.

NAKED LUNCH • KEY WEST

Eat naked! So many naked partiers at the Garden of Eden were having pizza delivered or bringing take-out, that the proprietors saw another opportunity. Just down the street, they opened Naked Lunch, perhaps the country's only freestanding clothing-optional restaurant. And the key word is optional. Dine in your clothes if you like. Or shed them and eat naked.

Although the object of the place is for you to feel accepted no matter what you want to do, there are limits, says the manager. No photographs are allowed. People aren't allowed to touch each other. Or themselves. And a sign in the restroom reads "No Sex."

Oh, well. Maybe the food's good.

Located at 4 Charles Street.

SLOPPY JOE'S • KEY WEST

Joe Russell was a boat captain, a fisherman, and a rumrunner. In the days of Prohibition, he operated illegal speakeasies, supplying the local freethinkers, including a writer known as Papa, with illicit bottles of liquor. It was during this time that Russell and Hemingway struck up their enduring friendship.

Russell became a legitimate bar owner on December 5, 1933—the day Prohibition ended. Leasing a rundown building on Greene Street from friend Tony Terracino for three dollars a week, he opened a bar and named it the Blind Pig. It was shabby and rowdy. There were pool tables, gambling, fifteen-cent whiskey, ten-cent shots of gin, and a long, curving bar. The name was briefly changed to the Silver Slipper when a dance floor was added, but the name seemed a bit delicate for such a raucous joint.

It was Hemingway who came up with the name Sloppy Joe's, and, huh, the name had nothing to do with the hygiene habits of its proprietor. It came, instead, from one of Papa's favorite bars in

The world-famous Sloppy Joe's Bar has been a Key West establishment since 1933 and was once a favorite haunt of Ernest Hemingway.
Courtesy of Amber K. Henderson

Cuba, which was owned by a man named Jose (Joe in Spanish) Garcia. That bar also sold seafood and ice and consequently the floor was always wet and … sloppy. The patrons nicknamed the bar Sloppy Joe's, and the name stuck. Hemingway wanted Russell to name his bar in tribute to that far-away favorite.

OK, we've already given you the story about the $1-a-week rent increase that prompted the move of Sloppy Joe's. It happened on May 5, 1937, and according to all reports, the patrons simply picked up their drinks and a chair or two and moved the bar into its new location. Hardly a drop was spilled, and the drinking continued on in the new establishment as if nothing untoward had occurred.

Situated on the corner of Greene and Duval streets, the new bar had jalousie doors that opened it to both streets. It had the town's longest bar and a gambling room. Life-sized paintings of prize fighters and a 119-pound sailfish caught by Hemingway served as wall decoration.

With ceiling fans churning the humid air above them, some of the country's most prominent freethinkers drank and wrote and fought here. Besides Hemingway, writer John Dos Pasos and artist Waldo Pierce were regular patrons.

If Hemingway were to return to his favorite haunt today, he'd feel as if he'd never left. Stepping through the jalousie doors, he'd find the same ceiling fans churning the humid air, and the bar, polished to a high shine by thousands of elbows, still the hub of activity. The only thing he'd find different—and perhaps a bit disturbing—is the collection of Hemingway memorabilia that now adorns the bar. And all those T-shirts for sale with his face on them!

Don't let it bother you, though, as you crawl through those

jalousie doors. Toss back a few shots in his name. Do the old man proud.

Need we say it? OK. Just in case you were drunk and missed it: located on the corner of Greene and Duval Streets.

Margaritaville

Yes, we know that Margaritaville is just a state of mind, but no place in the world exemplifies that funky state of fugue better than Key West and the Florida Keys. Besides, when Jimmy Buffett wrote the song, he wasn't just searching for his lost shaker of salt; he was searching for his lost season in Key West!

It's easy to lose yourself here. Stepping off the mainland and into the Keys is like entering a whole other dimension. Forget racing down multi-laned highways to your next destination. There's only one way in and one way out, and if the guy ahead of you ain't in a hurry, then neither are you.

And, believe us, he ain't gonna be in a hurry. The Keys run on island time—that is to say that time is irrelevant. Rise at your leisure. Eat when you're hungry. Loll in the sun with a margarita in your hand. And when the day is done, join us at the end of the world and celebrate the setting of the sun.

Life's a party, man. Live it.

Florida's Official Dessert

No tour of Florida would be complete without a word about Key lime pie, the official dessert of Key West. The history of that delectable confection of sweet and sour deliciousness dates back to the late 1800s, when a lack of refrigeration made milk a scarcity. Enterprising cooks improvised, however, using available ingredients, and came up with a dessert so luscious that almost two hundred years later, it's served around the world.

No one agrees about who exactly first came up with the original Key lime pie recipe, but everyone agrees on the ingredients. Ingredient number one was Borden's canned sweetened condensed milk, invented around 1858 and popular because it needed no refrigeration.

Ingredient number two in the original Key lime pie recipe was Key lime juice. Key limes, which came to the Keys from Malaysia in the 1500s, are different from the big green limes you usually see in your local grocery store, which are actually Persian limes. Key limes are small and greenish-yellow in color. They are tarter and juicier than Persian limes.

An egg or four was added to the mixture. Into a pastry shell it went. Bake a few minutes. Pile meringue on top, and pop back into the oven until the meringue turns a glistening gold. Voila! Key lime pie.

Because the high acidic content of Key lime juice was enough to curdle the condensed milk and allow the filling to set, an uncooked version of the pie was also popular.

Today's Key lime pie recipes differ a bit from the original, most specifically because an unfortunate 1926 hurricane wiped out the Key limes in Florida. Growers replanted Persian limes, which are easier to pick and transport. The only fresh Key limes are found in backyards these days. A bottled version of Key lime juice is available, however, and this is what most cooks now use.

Another difference is the piecrust. Most Key lime pies now come in a graham cracker crust instead of a traditional pie shell. And, fears of salmonella have some recipes leaving out the eggs in uncooked versions.

Key lime recipes abound. Here's one we've found that seems the closest to the original recipe:

INGREDIENTS:
4 egg yolks
4 egg whites
1 can Borden's sweetened condensed milk
1/2 cup fresh or bottled Key lime juice
1-2 tablespoons of sugar
1/4 teaspoon of cream of tartar
9-inch deep dish pastry pie shell

Mix egg yolks, milk, and lime juice in a bowl. Bake pie shell in 325° oven for 10-12 minutes, until golden brown. Pour mixture into crust and bake at 325° for 10-15 minutes.

Meanwhile:

Beat egg whites with sugar and cream of tartar until mixture peaks. Remove pie from oven, and pile on the meringue. Return to oven and bake until meringue is golden brown.

Now, examine that recipe carefully. Nowhere in there do you see green food coloring, right? Right. True Key lime pie is creamy yellow in color, not green. So the next time you ask for Key lime pie and you're served that garish green version, send it back, and find another restaurant. That one knows nothing about real Key lime pie!

Jubilee!

If you're visiting the northern Gulf coast area and hear this cry, grab a gig and the largest bucket you can find—heck, grab two—and follow the crowd to the beach. There you'll find an orgy of seafood wallowing right up on shore.

Wondering why these tasty creatures would throw themselves at your feet? It ain't because they like you. They're trying to get a breath of fresh air. A jubilee is a natural phenomenon where a specific series of conditions causes a stratification of low-oxygen water inside the bay. Most fish can swim above this low oxygen, but the bottom-dwellers, such as flounder and shellfish, are pushed to the shore as the low-oxygen water moves toward them.

So, next time you visit, look for a cloudy day with a gentle east wind, a calm bay surface, and a rising tide. There's just one catch: Jubilees usually happen between midnight and dawn, but a little loss of sleep is a small price to pay—both for the seafood and the fun!

Strange But True Characters

Florida has its share of notable people who have made major contributions to the state's, and even the nation's, culture. Here are just a few and the things they made famous.

ERNEST F. COE

As a youngster, Ernest Coe loved the outdoors, and as an adult, he loved exploring the Everglades. On one of those trips, he was shocked to learn of rare birds being killed, and rare or unusual orchids being taken from their natural habitat.

Coe was convinced that if something wasn't done, many species of animals and plants would soon be extinct. In 1928, he conceived his plans for a national park to be located within the lower Everglades. He created the Tropical

A visit to the Everglades will include a stop at the Ernest F. Coe Visitor Center.
Courtesy of Everglades National Park

Everglades National Park Association and appealed to notable Floridians to join the cause. Despite considerable resistance by legislators who failed to see the merits of Coe's vision, President Roosevelt signed the enabling act for Everglades National Park on May 30, 1934, though it would take another thirteen years to acquire the land and define the boundaries of the new park.

When the National Park was dedicated in 1947, it would have seemed that Coe would have every reason to celebrate, but he was disappointed that the final boundaries enclosed a smaller area than originally proposed. He insisted that without the upper part of Key Largo, the reef, and part of the Big Cypress, the park wouldn't have enough water supply to survive. Not until after his death were his arguments found to have merit. Everglades National Park was expanded, the reef tract gained protection with the creation of Biscayne National Park and the Florida Keys National Marine Sanctuary, and Big Cypress was designated as a national preserve.

Coe's efforts are remembered at the Ernest F. Coe Visitor Center in Homestead. A stop here will include a brief introductory film on the park, two movies on hurricanes, and a wildlife film for children.

HENRY FLAGLER

Anyone who has visited Florida has heard the name Henry Flagler. Throughout the state, there are streets, roads, and avenues named in his honor. There's a beach and town named for him. There's a Flagler Museum, a Flagler County, a Flagler Auditorium, and a Flagler Hospital. And in the middle of Biscayne Bay, on a tiny speck of an island, there is the Flagler

Memorial, a sixty-foot obelisk erected in his honor by Miami developer Carl Fisher.

Florida has good reason for all this honoring. Flagler, a railroad magnate, not only helped to develop the small town of St. Augustine, but by the extension of his railroad through the state, he also single-handedly kick-started the state's phenomenal growth—and its subsequent tourism industry.

Flagler's love affair with Florida began in St. Augustine. As a partner in the Standard Oil Company, Flagler visited that fair city and was charmed with the town and its climate. He moved there in 1883 and immediately began developing it to fit his family's needs. Dissatisfied with the accommodations and facilities, he built two huge hotels, a hospital, a water works, electric and sewer facilities, and a home for his family.

Henry Flagler is honored throughout Florida for his significant contributions to the state.
Courtesy of the State Archives of Florida

While there, he also entered the railroad business by rebuilding a small railroad. He must have liked this business, for he extended his railway into Palm Beach, where he built schools, churches, hospitals, fire stations, and utilities.

Strange But True Characters

This was as far as he planned to go, and for years he resisted the plea of Miamian Julia Tuttle to extend his railroad further south. Until the winter of 1894. An unexpected freeze hit the St. Augustine area, killing the orange crop and irritating Flagler, who preferred warm weather. When Julia Tuttle shipped him a branch of orange blossoms picked from her orchard the day of the freeze, Flagler decided that he would take his railroad to Miami. Indeed, he would extend it all the way to Key West.

This Key West dream of his became an obsession. So eager was he to build his railroad that he used his own money for the entire construction, which began in 1905. An enormous undertaking, the project became known as Flagler's Folly.

To begin, Flagler first had to obtain the land from donation, lease, or purchase. Because there was no land transportation in the Keys, the railroad was literally built from the sea. Flagler employed many ships dedicated to transporting supplies and materials for the project. He leased or purchased most of the heavy marine equipment available on the East Coast. At times, he even built his own equipment. Since the project would involve bridges over vast areas of water, he had large floating concrete mixers built for their construction.

Flagler set up camps all down the Keys, with construction going on in numerous areas at the same time. He wanted to lay as much track as possible as quickly as possible in the northern Keys, so he would be able to transport supplies and materials by train to the lower areas. The immediate goal was to first extend the railroad to Knight's Key, one of the middle keys, and set up from there to connect to Key West.

The first train arrived in Knight's Key on January 20, 1908, and a twice-daily schedule was quickly established. In anticipation of the difficult construction over the last area, which included a seven-mile expanse over water, a seaport city was also established, with a station capable of handling two trains, docks for two small steam ships, a hotel boat, a customs office, and a post office.

Work on the seven-mile Flagler Viaduct began in the spring of 1909. Joseph Meredith, the project leader, died that year, and the Keys were hit by a hurricane that wiped out most of the equipment being used in construction. Despite these setbacks, construction pushed on. It took three years, but finally, on January 22, 1912, the 82-year-old Flagler rode into Key West in his private rail car.

"Now I can die happy," he said. "My dream is fulfilled." He died the next year.

So now you see why there're so many Flagler monuments in Florida. The man gave a huge portion of his life and his fortune to the state. It's estimated that with all the developments he funded and the building of the railroad, Flagler spent about $50 million— about one-third the value of the entire state of Florida at the time.

By the 1930s, interest in rail travel was flagging (pun intended), and Flagler's railroad hit hard times, declaring bankruptcy in 1932. On Labor Day 1935, the death blow struck in the form of a powerful hurricane that killed hundreds in the Keys and wiped out forty miles of the railroad.

Instead of rebuilding the railroad, the state bought the railroad's right of way for pennies on the dollar, with the idea to construct a highway for automobiles. The original Overseas Highway, constructed using much of Flagler's railroad foundation, was completed in 1938. Construction on the present Overseas Highway, which runs parallel to the old highway, was completed in 1982.

If you're interested in learning more about Flagler and his struggle to build his folly, visit the Flagler Station and Overseas Railway Historium, located at the corner of Caroline and Margaret Streets in Key West.

Dr. John Gorrie

Florida can probably thank John Gorrie for its phenomenal growth. Without him, the place would just be too hot to live in. You see, Gorrie is credited with inventing air conditioning. In 1842, the Apalachicola physician was searching for a way to lower the fevers of hospital patients. The method he invented, using compressed gas to heat air and radiating coils to then cool and distribute it, is the principle used in today's refrigeration.

Dr. John Gorrie, Floridian physician and humanitarian, is known as the father of air conditioning and refrigeration.
Courtesy of Florida State Parks

Gorrie's first attempts consisted of placing bowls of ice around the hospital with a fan circulating the air. Ice was expensive because it had to be brought by boat from the northern lakes. So Gorrie set about to make artificial ice. Using his knowledge of compressed gases and steam engines, he eventually produced a machine that made ice in small quantities. He finally relinquished his medical practice to allow time to pursue his refrigeration projects.

Gorrie's first public showing of his invention was on Bastille Day in 1850, when he served ice-chilled champagne for the French Consul at the Mansion House Hotel. He was granted patents for his work in 1850 and 1851. Dr. Gorrie never realized any financial return on his work, but it continued, thanks to numerous other scientists that followed him. The National Academy of Engineers has recognized their cumulative effort as the tenth greatest achievement of the twentieth century.

The original machines, as well as Gorrie's scientific articles, are on display at the Smithsonian in Washington, D.C., and at the John Gorrie Museum, located at 46 Sixth Street in Apalachicola.

DR. BENJAMIN GREEN

Benjamin Green, a Miami physician, made a major contribution to the military and to Florida culture with the invention of a suntan cream to help WWII GIs suffering disabling sunburns in the South Pacific. As an Army chemist, Green developed a thick petroleum jelly with red dye that absorbed some of the sun's rays. When he returned home, he began experimenting with other lotions to block out the sun, cooking his concoctions on his wife's stove and testing them on his own bald head. He created a creamy cocoa butter mixture which he later called Coppertone; it caught on, and the rest is history.

ERNEST HEMINGWAY

Key West's most famous resident was perhaps Ernest "Papa" Hemingway. The great writer visited the island in 1928 and fell in love with it. Living in a small apartment over the local Ford dealership, he wrote *A Farewell To Arms*, which was published in 1929.

Papa married into money, and his wife's uncle, knowing how much he loved Key West, bought the couple a home on Whitehead Street. Wife Pauline, over Ernest's vehement protest, promptly added a swimming pool, Key West's first.

For ten years, Ernest Hemingway lived and wrote in Key West. Today, thousands of visitors come to see his home every year.
Courtesy of the Florida Keys & Key West Monroe County Tourist Development Council

Papa spent ten years in Key West, writing hard and drinking harder. Despite spending much of his time in a drunken stupor, he was able to pen such masterpieces as *For Whom The Bell Tolls*, *Death in the Afternoon*, and *To Have And Have Not*.

After Pauline divorced him, it's said that Hemingway dumped a load of papers at Sloppy Joe's, his favorite watering hole, and headed out to Cuba.

Today, his home is open to the public, with two most notable attractions for our Strange But True Florida tour. First, is the proliferation of six-toed cats that run free around the estate. There're fifty or more of these inbred kitties, which may have six or more toes.

The other most interesting point is the cat's drinking fountain. The top of the fountain is a large old olive jar that Papa brought home from Cuba. The bottom, though, ah, the bottom! That's a urinal from Sloppy Joe's that Papa, in one of his notorious drunken fits, ripped up and brought home for his beloved kitties to drink from. Horrified, Pauline tried to disguise the pissoir, to no avail, with decorative tile. Hemingway kept the house and visited periodically until his death by suicide in 1961.

Located at 907 Whitehead Street.

Spontaneous Human Combustion

Over the past three hundred years, there have been more than two hundred reports of Spontaneous Human Combustion, a phenomenon where a person bursts into flames and burns to ashes for no apparent reason. One such report concerns an incident in a well-known Florida town, St. Petersburg.

It seems that Mary Hardy Reeser, a 67-year-old widow, spontaneously combusted while casually sitting in her easy chair on July 1, 1951. Her neighbors went to check on her the following morning, and when they tried the doorknob, they found it hot to the touch. When they were able to get into her home, they found Mrs. Reeser's remains in a blackened circle four feet in diameter. All that was left of her was a small section of her backbone, a shrunken skull roughly the size of a baseball, and one foot in a black satin slipper just beyond the dark circle.

Seeking a rational explanation, police reported that Mrs. Reeser most likely caught her nightgown on fire, probably from a cigarette. But one medical examiner stated that the 3,000° heat needed to melt the body should have destroyed the apartment as well. Beyond ceiling and upper walls covered with soot, damage was minimal.

The scene of this truly strange occurrence can no longer be seen, but an account of it is available in Michael Harrison's *Fire From Heaven*, published in 1976.

Miscellaneous Miscellany

Here are some more points of strangeness on our strange but true tour:

It's the Law!

Better watch your step in Strange But True Florida. You never know when the long arm of the law might reach out and nab you for breaking one of these strange but true laws.

1. It's illegal for a single woman to parachute on Sunday. She can be arrested, fined, and/or jailed. But, officer, we were flying through the Bermuda Triangle when ....

2. It's illegal for women to fall asleep under a hair dryer. If you do, both you and the salon owner can be fined. I'm awake, really!

3. A woman can be fined—only after death—for being electrocuted in a bathtub while using beautification utensils. Sure, judge, the check's in the mail.

4. You cannot fart in a public place after 6:00 p.m. on Thursdays. Any other time, let 'er rip!

5. It's considered an offense to shower naked. Saves on laundry bills, though.

6. If you leave your elephant tied to a parking meter, you must feed the meter, just as you would with a car. Hold off feeding the elephant, though, unless you have a really big poop bag.

7. It's illegal to have sex with a porcupine. Painful, too.

8. Men may not be seen publicly in any kind of strapless gown. Oh, Lord! Don't tell 'em about Key West!

9. Pigs are not allowed on the beach in Miami. Nope. We're going to leave that one alone.

10. When having sex in Florida, only the missionary position is legal. Oops!

11. In Tampa, women may not expose their breasts while topless dancing. Really, officer. It was a wardrobe malfunction.

12. Also in Tampa, lap dances must be given at least six feet away from a patron. Honest, officer. She slipped!

13. In Daytona Beach, it's unlawful to swim in the Atlantic Ocean while intoxicated. Must be why Fort Lauderdale is the Spring Break Capital of the World.

14. It's illegal to change clothes in your car in Destin. Note to Superman: Phone booths are permitted.

15. It's illegal to molest a Key deer. See #10 above.

16. It's illegal to sing in public while wearing a swimsuit. Huh.

17. In Miami, it's illegal to molest garbage cans. Oh, yuck. That's just nasty!

18. Corrupting the public morals is a misdemeanor. Like I said, officer, it was a wardrobe malfunction!

19. It's illegal to commit any "unnatural" acts with another person. Define unnatural.

20. In Seaside, all homes must have a white picket fence and a two-story porch. Guess that means a double-wide is out?

Towns of Note

We'll conclude our tour of Strange But True Florida with a few of the state's strangely notable towns.

CASSADAGA • VOLUSIA COUNTY

No doubt about it. Cassadaga is a weird town. It was founded at the end of the nineteenth century by George Colby, an Iowa medium, who claimed he was guided there by three spirit guides to found a psychic center. Colby's center, which is now known as the Cassadaga Spiritualist Camp, was completed in 1898 and quickly became the focal point for spiritualists, those claiming to have supernatural abilities, including clairvoyance and the ability to speak with the dead.

Today, the town remains much as it was in the early days.

Miscellaneous Miscellany

Small cottages line both paved and dirt roads. There's the Cassadaga Hotel and a post office, and not much more. Eerily quiet, it's a place where its one hundred or so mediums, psychics, spiritualists, and astrologers work and live without interference.

You won't find tarot cards here. Or crystal balls, or hypnosis. They're not allowed. But for $40 to $65, you can get a spiritual reading or receive psychic counseling by one of the camp's forty mediums. You may even find someone who can contact the great beyond for you. Perhaps get in touch with Aunt Dodie; ask her what's the deal with leaving it all to crazy cousin Joe.

Weird? By all means. But a fitting stop on our tour through Strange But True Florida.

CLEWISTON • HENDRY COUNTY

Most of the country's sugar is grown in the counties south of Lake Okeechobee. Clewiston lies in the heart of this sugar cane center and so has earned the nickname the "Sweetest Town in America."

EATONVILLE • ORANGE COUNTY

Founded in 1887, Eatonville was the country's first incorporated black town. It was the first black community with a charter, mayor, city council, and town marshal.

Eatonville was the birthplace and home to noted author Zora Neale Hurston, who wrote of her pride in her hometown and the part it played in American history. Today, Eatonville is a predominately black community with a population of about two thousand.

GIBSONTON • HILLSBOROUGH COUNTY

During the heydays of the roadside tourist attractions, freak shows were a big draw. The people who starred in these shows often wintered in the small town of Gibsonton, and after the shows closed, many retired here.

Walking down the streets of the town could be quite interesting. It wasn't unusual to see the bearded lady, the world's tallest man, or lobster boy, born with a genetic condition that joined his fingers and toes into flipper-like appendages.

Although most have either passed away or moved, the town is still well-known by its nickname: Freak City, U.S.A.

OPA LOCKA • MIAMI-DADE COUNTY

Driving into Opa Locka, you might think you've taken a wrong turn and somehow ended up in Arabia. In fact, the entire town was built on one man's idealized version of *The Arabian Nights*, featuring Moorish architectural

Opa Locka's City Hall, as well as other buildings in the city, features domes and minarets inspired by Moorish architecture. Courtesy of the City of Opa Locka

characteristics, such as onion domes, elaborate minarets, and bright colors.

Constructed on the site known as Opatishawockalocka by the Tequesta Indians, the town was a planned community built by multimillionaire Glenn Curtiss, who had recently seen the 1924 movie *The Thief of Baghdad* and was fascinated by the strange architecture he saw in it.

After first shortening the town's name, Curtiss set about building a Moorish city in the middle of the Florida Everglades. All the buildings sported domes and minarets, and even the streets carried the theme, with names such as Ali Baba Avenue, Cairo Lane, and Harem Avenue. At the center of the town was the Opa Locka City Hall, rising like a shimmering oasis from the Florida sands.

Although many of the original Opa Locka buildings are run down, several, including the city hall, have been restored to their former glory, and twenty are listed on the National Register of Historic Places.

Romeo • Marion County

So what else are ya gonna name a town that's just down the road from Juliette?

Seaside • Walton County

This quaint-looking coastal town, with its brick-paved streets and mandatory white picket fences, is so stereotypically Americana that it was chosen as the backdrop for the 1996 Jim Carrey movie *The Truman Show*, about a man living in a fake town.

The white-picketed city of Seaside served as the backdrop for *The Truman Show*, which starred Jim Carrey.
Courtesy of Steven Brooke

The little town has received international attention as a community strictly planned, from the small size, to the color and style of the homes and businesses, to the mandate that all homes have a picket fence and a two-story porch.

TWO EGG • JACKSON COUNTY

When the unusual name was chosen for this unassuming little town, we're sure folks never expected anyone to notice. Certainly, they never anticipated that the name would draw busloads of curious tourists. Or that as a result, the Lawrence Grocery Store, the heart of this crossroads town, would do a brisk business in Two Egg souvenirs. Or that the town sign would have to be continually replaced because someone was always stealing it. They didn't anticipate it. But they're dealing with it.

So how did the town get that name? According to legend, the town was named by traveling salesmen. It seems that when visiting the local general store, the salesmen observed customers bartering for two eggs worth of tobacco, sugar, flour, snuff, and other goods. The salesmen started calling the place a two-egg town, and the name stuck. Huh.

Art Deco

The art deco movement of the 1920s and 1930s was tailor-made for South Florida. The pastel colors and hyper-modern architecture seemed to exemplify the carefree attitude that, despite all the glitz and glam, permeated the area.

The art deco hotels that populate Miami's Ocean Drive and Collins Avenue, now known as the historic Art Deco District, were built during this party era. Entrepreneurs Carl Fisher and John Collins wanted to make it into a playground for the rich and famous of the day. And they succeeded.

The first buildings were completed during Prohibition, and the area soon became associated not only with the multimillionaires that its developers hoped to attract, but also with speakeasies, gambling, and characters such as Al Capone. By the 1980s, the area had deteriorated into a slum and had become a center for drug trafficking.

Soon after, however, the television show *Miami Vice* put the spotlight on the city, and many partially credit its influence with the sudden revival of the South Beach area. The major share of the credit, though, goes to the Miami Design Preservation League, which raised funds for the restoration of the area's buildings.

Today, the art deco hotels have been meticulously restored and are established as the Art Deco National Historic District, the only such designation in the U.S. The rich and famous have returned, and Sobe (short for South Beach) has become known as the American Riviera.